PENGUIN BOOKS

HAPPY DAYS WITH THE NAKED CHEF

'Absolutely yummy . . . Who would have thought of serving pork fillet on a bed of rhubarb? It looks so scrumptious that I want to dash off and cook it now' *Daily Telegraph*

'Twelve-year-olds will like it . . . women will like it . . . men will like it . . . Problem solved' *The Times*

'Don't be fooled into thinking this is the Naked Chef without the mockney banter - it's "Gordon Bennett" and "scrumptious, mate" all the way through . . . The food is simply explained and superbly presented, and it makes you want to cook every dish' *Daily Express*

'Great, fabulous. There's some really hot lips and some scrumptious recipes that really hit the spot. Just enjoy yourself, get stuck in, happy days' *Spectator*

'Jamie shows you how to create pukka food that's fresh, funky and easy to cook' *OK!*

'Well over 100 new recipes to get stuck into . . . we're pleased to say there's even more enthusiasm in this book than in his previous two' *Heat*

'Great for sparking kids' interest' *She*

'Full of great recipes for all occasions' *Homes & Ideas*

'His third book, *Happy Days with the Naked Chef,* will delight those legions of fans who are already converts to his ideas for classy, modern food' *Birmingham Post*

'Bubbly, sociable and passionate about food, Jamie brings us lots of recipes for every occasion . . . making cooking accessible and getting the most out of ingredients with the minimum fuss' *Eastern Daily Press*

'Jamie Oliver is quite a bit more than a pretty face and after his third cookbook most will conclude he is not just a flash in the proverbial starry pan either' *Knaresborough Post*

'*Happy Days with the Naked Chef* has lots of interesting, must-try recipes, and reminds you that he is pretty nifty in the kitchen' *Glasgow Evening Times*

'Get set for another helping of sexy TV chef Jamie Oliver – and don't be surprised if you want afters!' *Plymouth Evening Herald*

'If cooking is the new rock and roll, 26-year-old chef Jamie Oliver is its brightest star' *Harrogate Advertiser*

'His most accessible cookery book yet . . . it's hard not to love the guy's style' *Church of England Newspaper*

ABOUT THE AUTHOR

Jamie Oliver started cooking at his parents' pub, the Cricketers, in Clavering, Essex, at the age of eight. He has worked with some of the top chefs in the country – including Antonio Carluccio and Gennaro Contaldo at the Neal Street Restaurant and Rose Gray and Ruth Rogers at the River Café – and is now running his new restaurant, Fifteen, in East London. He lives in London with his wife, Jools, and their daughters, Poppy Honey and Daisy Boo.

Happy Days with the Naked Chef

Jamie Oliver

with photographs by David Loftus

PENGUIN BOOKS

PENGUIN BOOKS

Published by the Penguin Group
Penguin Books Ltd, 80 Strand, London WC2R 0RL, England
Penguin Putnam Inc., 375 Hudson Street, New York, New York 10014, USA
Penguin Books Australia Ltd, Ringwood, Victoria, Australia
Penguin Books Canada Ltd, 10 Alcorn Avenue, Toronto, Ontario, Canada M4V 3B2
Penguin Books India (P) Ltd, 11, Community Centre, Panchsheel Park,
New Delhi - 110 017, India
Penguin Books (NZ) Ltd, Cnr Rosedale and Airborne Roads,
Albany, Auckland, New Zealand
Penguin Books (South Africa) (Pty) Ltd, 5 Watkins Street,
Denver Ext 4, Johannesburg 2094, South Africa

Penguin Books Ltd, Registered Offices: 80 Strand, London WC2R 0RL, England

www.penguin.com

First published by Michael Joseph 2001
Published in Penguin Books 2003
2

Set in 10/15 pt Akzidenz Grotesk Light
Typeset by Rowland Phototypesetting Ltd, Bury St Edmunds, Suffolk

Printed in Great Britain by Butler & Tanner Ltd, Frome, Somerset

A CIP catalogue record for this book is available from the British Library

Get closer to the Naked Chef at www.penguin.co.uk/jamieoliver
Exclusive features, interviews, video clips, recipes,
competitions and all the latest news
Or go to Jamie's personal site at
www.jamieoliver.com

CONTENTS

Dedicated to:

Little Henners

Jakey Bakey

the cooks of tomorrow

Gordon Bennett

– last year was busy but this one has been doolally! Here I am in Cornwall writing this introduction, whilst being clicked at by photographers in bushes. Before you think it, I'm not getting tired of cooking. I think I'm even more obsessed! It's become a weekly occurrence to wake up after being bashed by my missus telling me that I've been muttering in my sleep about sweet red onions and fields of herbs – don't remember it, but it wouldn't surprise me. It didn't stop her marrying me – yep, Mr and Mrs Oliver we are now – and I think she still likes me!

On the big day itself we were up at 5 a.m. cooking with my dad, Gennaro my London 'dad', my best man Bender the Aussie, and my chef mates from Monte's. What a fantastic day. All I wanted to see was our best friends and family really tucking in and having a laugh, so for starters I had lots of different tapas and antipasti, fresh bread and big plates of Parma ham, bresaola and salamis from Italy. Little bowls of chutneys and sauces went with them and it worked. Everyone was tucking in, passing stuff around, and from the top table it was a fantastic sight – definitely the feast of the year. For the main course we had whole wild salmon stuffed with loadsa herbs and baked with a little white wine and olive oil. This was served with lemon and basil mayonnaise, boiled potatoes dug up from Dad's garden that morning, and nice green salad. For dessert, the sweetest strawberries and some mascarpone cream. Lovely. So simple but perfect for a summer wedding.

Jools and my mum still act as a fantastic grounding for my cooking. After nine years of Jools hating everything about cooking I realized recently that I was being too honest about her attempts — no matter how I put it, she considered it a bit of a knockback, so I lied and said 'It's fantastic, babe!' to whatever she cooked for me. Since then she hasn't stopped cooking and has naturally got better and better. She now doesn't mind discussing the finer details and she's doing loadsa cooking at home. Everyone likes to feel that they're good at something and cooking is no exception. I do find Jools's opinions massively helpful in writing a book which must be accessible to everyone because if she can do it, so can you. What I've really enjoyed recently is cooking together — before, she used to heckle me from the stairs, which really used to wind me up. Now we're quite a good team in the kitchen and it means we get things done quicker.

Over the last year or so, I've done quite a bit of travelling which has been very inspiring on the old food front — Australia, New Zealand, America and Japan. Every country blew me away with a handful of genius dinners. There was the odd shocker, one of which came in the form of a bullock's bollocks in the US. And cod semen (disguised as chicken) in Japan — it's a delicacy over there and I was the guest of honour so I got the biggest portion. It tasted all right, but it just felt wrong.

I finished off the year by taking over as consultant chef at Monte's in Sloane Street, London. It has been a real challenge and education to launch a restaurant from scratch, following in the footsteps of chef Alain Ducasse, and I'm really happy with the young team that works for me in the kitchen, headed up by Bender the Aussie. And apart from that, we're busy. It's been great to carry on writing seasonal menus using the best produce while still searching for the perfect restaurant site of my own.

People keep asking me if the success of the books and the programmes has changed me and all my thoughts about food. Well, I think as a person I haven't really changed apart from having to grow up a bit. But from the feedback I've had in letters and e-mails to my website (www.jamieoliver.com) I definitely think I've got more of an idea about what the average person wants to cook at home. I've written *Happy Days* with this in mind.

I feel like this book has moved naturally on from the first two as it's still focusing on reality: being able to buy the best ingredients you can. You know what I mean, simple, comforting, homely food is still what it's all about. Foodwise, this year has been very creative for me and, as you'll see in the book, I've come up with loads of new recipes, as well as some really cool new chapters that I'm very excited about. The most important one is Kids' Club, which is all about getting parents to capture their kids' imaginations to get them involved and interested in food. Then there's Quick Fixes, which is all about quick, tasty dinners — ideal for when you get in late after a hard day's work. Comfort Grub is all your old favourites and some new ideas — to be eaten while snuggled up in front of the TV.

I'm really proud of *Happy Days* — to me it feels more like a diary than a cookbook, as it's my memories of the last couple of years and because of that it's very eclectic, with little fusions and ideas from my travels. I've included some classic recipes as well as putting a twist on others to reflect my personal taste. But, hey, that's what it's all about.

Cooking … happy days! Love Jamie. x

Cupboard Stuff

HERBS The question is why is a twenty-six-year-old full-blooded Essex boy devoting two precious pages of his beloved book to herbs? I respect the fact that my lovely missus thinks I'm crackers with my obsession for the fragrant leaves, but quite frankly they're cool – not just cool, but very cool. If there were no herbs in this world I would give up cooking tomorrow; how boring would cooking be? With herbs you can completely transform a dish, make it heartier, lighter or more fragrant, and marry together all sorts of dishes that may never have worked without them … To grow them and have them right there at the kitchen window at their freshest is a cook's dream; to run out to get herbs to bash up in a pestle and mortar and smear over a nice piece of lamb with a little oil is the best.

If you're a real connoisseur of herbs you'll probably meet my mate Jekka along the way, be it at Chelsea Flower Show or at a festival. She's amazing, completely potty about herbs, nurturing and growing the most fantastic herb cuttings and seeds from all over the world, with looks, tastes and smells that you've never experienced before. It's like heaven to me; I'm already planning my herb garden in my non-existent garden. I've only known her for a short amount of time but that's the great thing about food or any passion really, it will always bring people together to become buddies.

All this little chapter is about is to say please try getting into herbs, they are a real trick to kick-starting your cooking. Not only that, but after a good gossip with Jekka, I was really shocked to find out that using herbs simply for flavouring is quite a new thing in the history of food. Different herbs were used as natural and accessible antiseptics that would aid digestion; herbs like sage can arrest the ageing process and can be found in some face creams, but originally sage was packed with meat to make it keep for much longer. Fennel, coriander, tarragon and dill are great for digestion and help break down cholesterol. Good old mint is an anti-inflammatory and stimulates the appetite. And rosemary is great for the liver and a great calming and stress-relieving herb. This is naming just a few, but the point is that even when you don't know it you're doing yourself a great deal of good when you use herbs in your cooking, so get stuck in and get out ya herbs.

COMFORT GRUB The idea of this chapter is to touch on a couple of those hearty, homely comfort grub dinners, like Toad in the Hole and a nice beef stew with 'Newkie Brown' ale and dumplings – meals for those lazy nights where you curl up in front of the telly and just chill out.

Comfort food can come from many countries with things like the ultimate chilli con carne, or the fluffiest American pancakes. With this chapter I wanted to reassure you that even though I'm a chef, I still get cravings for a good old fish finger buttie or sticky sausage and cheese bap with brown sauce. The one thing all these recipes have in common is normally memories of childhood; enjoying company round the dinner table, or in my case, coming home shivering and wet from playing footie with the boys and being ordered to change out of my wet clothes into my dressing-gown before being given a steaming bowl of chilli with a jacket potato and a lob of guacamole and yoghurt. Remember: Don't eat to live, but live to eat. That's what it's all about!

Toad in the Hole

SERVES 4

sunflower oil • 8 large good-quality sausages • 4 sprigs of
fresh rosemary • 2 large red onions, peeled and sliced •
2 cloves of garlic, peeled and finely sliced • 2 knobs of butter
• 6 tablespoons balsamic vinegar • 1 level tablespoon
good-quality vegetable stock powder or 1 vegetable stock cube

FOR THE BATTER

285ml/½ pint milk • 115g/4oz plain flour • a pinch
of salt • 3 eggs

Mix the batter ingredients together, and put to one side. I like the batter to go huge so the key thing is to have an appropriately-sized baking tin – the thinner the better – as we need to get the oil smoking hot.

Put 1cm/just under ½ inch of sunflower oil into a baking tin, then place this on the middle shelf of your oven at its highest setting (240–250°C/475°F/gas 9). Place a larger tray underneath it to catch any oil that overflows from the tin while cooking. When the oil is very hot, add your sausages. Keep your eye on them and allow them to colour until lightly golden.

At this point, take the tin out of the oven, being very careful, and pour your batter over the sausages. Throw a couple of sprigs of rosemary into the batter. It will bubble and possibly even spit a little, so carefully put the tin back in the oven, and close the door. Don't open it for at least 20 minutes, as Yorkshire puddings can be a bit temperamental when rising. Remove from the oven when golden and crisp.

For the onion gravy, simply fry off your onions and garlic in the butter on a medium heat for about 5 minutes until they go sweet and translucent. You could add a little thyme or rosemary if you like. Add the balsamic vinegar and allow it to cook down by half. At this point, I do cheat a little and add a stock cube or powder. You can get some good ones in the supermarkets now that aren't full of rubbish. Sprinkle this in and add a little water. Allow to simmer and you'll have a really tasty onion gravy. Serve at the table with your Toad in the Hole, mashed potatoes, greens and baked beans or maybe a green salad if you're feeling a little guilty!

Good Old Steak and Guinness Pie

This is nice and easy to make as all you have to do is put a puff pastry lid on top of a dish filled with your stewed meat. I never serve anything else with these pies but if you want to, boiled potatoes and steamed greens always hit the spot.

SERVES 6

680g/1½lb stewing beef, diced • sea salt and freshly ground black pepper • 2 heaped tablespoons flour • olive oil • 1 onion, peeled and roughly chopped • 1 large carrot, peeled and roughly chopped • 4 sticks of celery, washed and roughly chopped • 2 parsnips, peeled and roughly chopped • 1 handful of fresh mixed herbs (rosemary, thyme and bay), leaves picked • 565ml/1 pint Guinness • 2 x 400g/14oz tins of tomatoes • 1 x 500g/1lb 2oz pack of puff pastry • 1 egg, beaten

Season your beef generously with salt and pepper, sprinkle with the flour and toss around until coated. Heat 2 or 3 lugs of olive oil in a large casserole-type pan and fry your meat, in 2 batches if need be, until golden brown. Add the onion and fry for 1 more minute, then add the carrot, celery, parsnips and herbs. Fry for a further 4 minutes then pour in your Guinness. Add the tinned tomatoes and bring to the boil. Stir around, then simmer for around 2 hours or until the meat is really tender. The sauce should be nice and thick with an intensely tasty flavour. Season. At this point you could serve it as a stew with mash, or it will keep really well for a good 5 days in the fridge (while improving in flavour at the same time).

To make the pies, preheat the oven to 190°C/375°F/gas 5. Put your meat filling into an appropriately-sized baking dish or dishes. I like to make small individual pies – any high-sided round ovenproof bowls are fine. Roll out your pastry, dusting with flour as you go, until 0.5cm/¼ inch thick. Cut out 6 circles about 1cm/½ inch bigger than the tops of your bowls. Brush the rims of your bowls with beaten egg, then place the pastry circles on top, squashing the excess pastry down the outside of the bowls to secure. Lightly score the top of the pastry in a criss-cross fashion and brush with more of the beaten egg. Bake in the middle of the preheated oven for 45 minutes until golden and bubbling.

Beef Stew with Newcastle Brown Ale and Dumplings

SERVES 6–8

1kg/2lb 3oz shin of beef (or use flank or neck), chopped into chunks • 3 tablespoons flour • olive oil • 3 red onions, peeled, halved and roughly sliced • 50g/1¾oz pancetta or smoked streaky bacon, chopped • 3 sticks of celery, chopped • 1 small handful of rosemary, leaves picked • 1.3 litres/2 pints Newcastle Brown ale • 2 parsnips, peeled and roughly chopped • 2 carrots, peeled and roughly chopped • 4 potatoes, peeled and roughly chopped • sea salt and freshly ground black pepper

FOR THE DUMPLINGS

225g/8oz self-raising flour • 115g/4oz butter • a good pinch of salt and pepper • 2 sprigs of rosemary, chopped

Season the beef, sprinkle with the flour and toss around until well coated. Heat up a frying pan until it is good and hot, add a little olive oil and fry the beef in 2 batches until nice and brown. Transfer the meat to a big casserole – one which is suitable to go on a hob – mixing in the flour that was left on the plate after coating it. Put the casserole on a medium heat, add the onions and pancetta, and cook until the onions are translucent and the pancetta has a bit of colour. Add your celery and rosemary. Now you can pour in your Newcastle Brown and 285ml/½ pint of water, adding your parsnips, carrots and potatoes. (Feel free to add whatever veg you like at this stage.) Bring to the boil, put a lid on, turn down the heat and leave it to simmer while you make the dumplings – which are choice.

Blitz the dumpling ingredients in a blender or rub between your fingers till you have a breadcrumb consistency, then add just enough water to make a dough that isn't sticky. Divide it into ping-pong-ball-sized dumplings and put these into the stew, dunking them under. Put the lid back on and leave it to cook for 2 hours. Taste it, season it as you like, and then serve the stew with some cavolo nero or other greens and loads of bread to mop up the juices.

Chilli con Carne

It's great to buy chuck steak for this recipe because you know exactly what quality of meat you're buying. Then simply cut it into pieces and pulse in a food processor until it resembles minced beef. I normally make double the amount of chilli needed so that I can divide the extra into sandwich bags, knotted at the top, for freezing. These bags can then be boiled for 15 minutes when needed.

SERVES 4

2 medium onions • 1 clove of garlic • olive oil • 2 level teaspoons chilli powder • 1 fresh red chilli, deseeded and finely chopped • 1 heaped teaspoon ground cumin (or crushed cumin seeds) • sea salt and freshly ground black pepper • 455g/1lb chuck steak, minced, or best minced beef • 200g/7oz sun-dried tomatoes, in oil • 2 x 400g/14oz tins of tomatoes • ½ a stick of cinnamon • 2 x 400g/14oz tins of red kidney beans, drained

To cook this I use a metal pan or casserole with a lid, which you can use on the hob and in the oven. If you are going to use the oven method (see below), then preheat the oven to 150°C/300°F/gas 2. Blitz the onions and garlic in a Magimix food processor until finely chopped, then fry in a little olive oil until soft. Add the chilli powder, fresh chilli, cumin and a little seasoning. Then add the minced chuck steak or beef and continue to cook, stirring, until it has browned. Blitz the sun-dried tomatoes in the food processor with enough oil from the jar to loosen into a paste. Add these to the beef with the tomatoes, cinnamon stick and a wineglass of water. Season a little more if need be.

Bring to the boil, cover with greaseproof paper and the lid, then either turn the heat down to simmer and cook for 1½ hours or transfer the pan to the oven for about 1½ hours. Add the tinned kidney beans 30 minutes before the end of the cooking time – they are already cooked and only need warming up.

This always tastes better if you cook it the day before (to give the flavours time to develop), so it's really handy if you've got friends coming round and don't want to be stuck in the kitchen. Just take it out of the fridge and warm it up – serve it with lots of fresh crusty bread, a nice tossed salad, and a big blob of natural yoghurt or guacamole.

My Favourite Curry Sauce

You will really like this curry – it's easy and fun to make. Two little tips are first, to use a Magimix or food processor to chop the onions and tomatoes as it makes less mess, it's really quick and will stop you crying! Second, get all your ingredients prepared and ready to go, then you can have the sauce finished in 15 minutes. Keep your eyes peeled for curry leaves – I'm trying to get supermarkets to stock them at the moment, but you can buy them from Indian or Asian delis. Get yourself a big bag of them, let them dry and they'll last for ages. If you really can't get them, do without, but it won't be quite the same.

SERVES 4

5 tablespoons vegetable oil • 2 teaspoons mustard seeds • 1 teaspoon fenugreek seeds • 3 fresh green chillies, deseeded and thinly sliced • 1 handful of curry leaves • 2 thumb-sized pieces of fresh ginger, peeled and coarsely grated • 3 onions, peeled and chopped • 1 teaspoon chilli powder • 1 teaspoon turmeric • 6 tomatoes, chopped • 1 x 400ml/14fl oz tin coconut milk • salt

FOR THE FISH VERSION

4 x 8oz/225g fresh haddock fillets, skinned and pin-boned • 1 knob of tamarind paste or 1 teaspoon tamarind syrup • optional: 1 large handful of baby spinach • optional: 1 good handful of fresh coriander, chopped

FOR THE CHICKEN VERSION

4 chicken breasts, sliced into 1cm/½ inch strips • 1 tablespoon coriander seeds, crushed

FOR THE VEGETARIAN VERSION

800g/1¾lb mixed vegetables, chopped (potatoes, courgettes, peppers, onions, sweet potatoes, spinach, chard, cauliflower, lentils, beans ... use your imagination)

Heat the oil in a pan, and when hot add the mustard seeds. Wait for them to pop, then add the fenugreek seeds, fresh green chillies, curry leaves and ginger. Stir and fry for a few minutes. Using a Magimix food processor, chop the onions and add to the same pan. Continue to cook for 5 minutes until the onion is light brown and soft, then add the chilli powder and turmeric. Using the same food processor, pulse the tomatoes and add these to the pan. Cook for a couple of minutes, then add 1 or 2 wineglasses of water and the coconut milk. Simmer for about 5 minutes until it has the consistency of double cream, then season carefully with salt.

Take this sauce as a base. To make the fish curry, add the fish and tamarind to the sauce and simmer for 6 minutes. Feel free to add some baby spinach and chopped coriander at the end of the cooking time. For the chicken version, stir-fry the chicken strips and coriander seeds until lightly coloured, then add to your sauce and simmer for 10 minutes. For the vegetarian version simply add all your veg to the sauce at the beginning when you add your onions. Continue to cook as normal and simmer until tender.

Lemon Rice

I've always wanted to know how Indian and Thai chefs make tasty rice. This is a great way to liven up plain rice but feel free to take it a step further by adding turmeric, like my Indian friend Das. Or hot it up with a little chilli powder. You can also fry some broken nuts, scramble in some eggs, try any ideas or flavours that you think are apt.

SERVES 4

455g/1lb basmati rice • 5 tablespoons vegetable oil •
2 tablespoons mustard seeds • 2 teaspoons urad dhal (small
dried split peas) • 1 handful of curry leaves • rind and
juice of 2 lemons • 1 bunch of fresh coriander, chopped •
sea salt and freshly ground black pepper

Throw the rice into boiling water, cook for 10 minutes and drain.

Heat the oil in a small frying pan, over a medium heat. Add the mustard seeds and as they begin to pop add the urad dhal, curry leaves and strips of lemon rind (remove these with a vegetable peeler). Leave to cook for 1 minute until the urad dhal and lemon peel are lightly coloured.

Add the drained steaming rice to a bowl and pour over the cooked spices, lemon juice and chopped coriander. Season to taste. Serve with a good curry (see page 32).

Coriander Chutney

400ml/4fl oz plain yoghurt • 1 bunch of fresh coriander, leaves
picked • 2–3 cloves of garlic • ½ a thumb-sized piece of ginger
• 2 green chillies, seeds removed • juice of ½ a lime • salt

Place all the ingredients in a food processor and blend until smooth. This will keep
in an airtight container for 2–3 days.

Lemon Pickle

2 teaspoons mustard seeds • 2 tablespoons olive oil • optional:
1 small handful of curry leaves • optional: 1 teaspoon urad dhal
(small dried split peas) • 1 teaspoon chilli powder • 4 tablespoons
wine vinegar • 2 lemons, washed, deseeded and chopped

Fry the mustard seeds in the hot oil. As they begin to pop add the curry leaves and
urad dhal. Lower the heat and add the chilli powder; cook until brown, then add the
vinegar. Stir in the lemon, remove from the heat and leave to cool. Can be stored
in the fridge for a week.

Fantastic Fish Finger Buttie

As a chef I always feel I shouldn't be eating something like a fish finger buttie – but you know what, I think that makes it taste even better. Here's what I do...

I remove about 4 fish fingers from the freezer and grill them on each side until crispy and golden. While that's happening, I butter 2 bits of nice soft white bread or a white roll, smearing one half generously with tomato ketchup. When the fish fingers are done, I remove them from the grill and place them on the bread smeared with ketchup. The most important bit is to put the other bit of bread on top and, using a little force, push down on your buttie which, for some reason, seems to make it taste even better. And that's it – all done.

I tend to eat one of these while I'm walking about at home and I always get told off by the missus for dropping bits everywhere. You'll notice from the picture that I've put a handful of rocket in the sandwich, which isn't really necessary but it does make it look a bit more posh. I was a bit embarrassed to tell the photographer he had to shoot a fish finger sandwich, so I told him it was 'lemon sole goujons' – what a prat I am! Be proud to eat fish fingers, that's what I say.

Sticky Sausage Bap with Melted Cheese and Brown Sauce

I used to have one of these every morning at 7 a.m. on the way to college at Westminster. Just get 3 half-decent snags (that's sausages to us southerners) and grill them until sticky and crispy on all sides. Remove to a plate, cut them in half, and line them up in the grill tray in the shape of your bap. Cover evenly with a good handful of grated mild Cheddar cheese and put back under the grill for the cheese to melt. Slice your bap in half, butter both sides, and smear outrageously with brown sauce. Using a knife, place your sausages and melted cheese on the brown sauce side of the bap. Then push the other side down on top of it and tuck in!

Pancakes USA Stylie

These American pancakes are great! Instead of being thin and silky like French crêpes, they are wonderfully fluffy and thick and can be made to perfection straight away. Simple, simple, simple — my Jools goes mad for them!

SERVES 2–4

3 large eggs • 115g/4oz plain flour • 1 heaped teaspoon baking powder • 140ml/5fl oz milk • a pinch of salt

First separate the eggs, putting the whites into one bowl and the yolks into another. Add the flour, baking powder and milk to the yolks and mix to a smooth thick batter. Whisk the whites with the salt until they form stiff peaks. Fold into the batter — it is now ready to use.

Heat a good non-stick pan on a medium heat. Pour some of your batter into the pan and fry for a couple of minutes until it starts to look golden and firm. At this point sprinkle your chosen flavouring (see below) on to the uncooked side before loosening with a spatula and flipping the pancake over. Continue frying until both sides are golden.

You can make these pancakes large or small, to your liking. You can serve them simply doused in maple syrup and even with some butter or crème fraîche. Or if you choose to sprinkle with a flavouring, try one of these...

fresh corn from the cob • crispy bacon or pancetta • blueberries • banana • stewed apple • grated chocolate • anything else you can imagine . . .

PS Blueberry pancakes (above) are great but you *must* try the corn pancakes. On one condition – you must use fresh corn. To do this, remove the outer leaves and carefully run a knife down the cob – this will loosen all the lovely pieces of corn – and sprinkle these raw over your pancake, before flipping it in the pan. I like to have some grilled bacon over my corn pancakes, drizzled with a little maple syrup. This sounds bloody horrid but it honestly tastes pukka!

QUICK FIXES This chapter is all about really fast tasty ways to eat good old chicken, steak, cod and salmon, time and minimal washing up being of the essence. I'm going to give you quick methods like frying or grilling, or my favourite, baking in the bag, which I started doing when Jools and I first moved to London six years ago – with me having been briefed by the lovely mother-in-law to 'look after my little baby'. We were completely skint, our kitchen was the size of an airing-cupboard and we were working opposite shifts to each other. I didn't want Jools to feed herself on ready meals so I found myself custom-making the fantastic 'Jamie Oliver dinners in a bag', involving the glorious tin-foil. I've got a thing about tin-foil – people must think either I'm a bit kinky because I use so much of it, or that I sponsor NASA!

I love making these little envelopes, or bags, with all the ingredients placed in the middle of them. What this means is that there's no washing up (just tin-foil in the bin), you don't have to use that much fat, just a little olive oil will do, and you can do pretty much any combination you like. But the great thing is that you cook your meat or your fish in the same bag as the vegetables and herbs, which, in return, gives you a healthy, homemade sauce which is great. The two baking-in-the-bag recipes I'm going to give you here use chicken, but you can do all kinds of fish, noodles, or a vegetarian bag.

What I would do for Jools was make up a combo at 4 p.m., as I was going off to work, and write with a marker pen '20 minutes at 200ºC', for example, on the foil. Even though Jools didn't like cooking, she never had a problem with cooking the bags.

Chicken Breast Baked in a Bag with Mushrooms, Butter, White Wine and Thyme

SERVES 2

2 x 200g/7oz skinless chicken breasts • 1 handful of dried
porcini • 255g/9oz mixed mushrooms, torn up • 1 large
wineglass of white wine • 3 large knobs of butter • 1 handful
of fresh thyme • 2 cloves of garlic, peeled and sliced

As this is for 2 people, I'm going to make a large envelope/bag to cook everything in. Using wide tin-foil, make your bag by placing 2 pieces on top of each other (about as big as 2 shoeboxes in length), folding 3 sides in and leaving 1 side open.

Preheat the oven to 220°C/425°F/gas 7. Mix everything together in a bowl, including the chicken. Place in your bag, with all the wine juice, making sure you don't pierce the foil. Close up the final edge, making sure the bag is tightly sealed and secure on all sides, and carefully slide it on to a roasting tray. Place the tray on a high heat on the hob for 1 minute to get the heat going, then bake in the middle of your preheated oven for 25 minutes.

Remove from the oven, place the bag on a big plate, take it to the table and break open the foil. Feel free to vary the recipe — things like grated parsnip, smoked bacon and red wine also work well.

Chicken Breast Baked in a Bag with Cannellini Beans, Leeks, Cream and Marjoram

SERVES 2

about 10 baby leeks, trimmed and washed • 2 x 200g/7oz skinless chicken breasts • 1 x 400g/14oz tin of cannellini beans, drained and washed • 1 clove of garlic, peeled and sliced • 1 small handful of fresh marjoram or oregano, leaves picked • 1 small wineglass of white wine • 140ml/5fl oz double cream • sea salt and freshly ground black pepper

As this is for 2 people, I'm going to make a large envelope/bag to cook everything in. Using wide tin-foil, make your bag by placing 2 pieces on top of each other (about as big as 2 shoeboxes in length), folding 3 sides in and leaving 1 side open.

Preheat the oven to 220°C/425°F/gas 7. Put the leeks into a pan and cook in boiling water for 2 minutes, just to soften. Drain and mix in a bowl with all the other ingredients, including the chicken, mushing a handful of the cannellini beans to a pulp in your hands. Season well, then place in your bag with all the creamy sauce, making sure you don't pierce the foil. Close up the final edge, making sure the bag is tightly sealed and secure on all sides, and carefully slide it on to a roasting tray. Place the tray on a high heat on the hob for 1 minute to get the heat going, then bake in the middle of your preheated oven for 25 minutes.

Remove from the oven, place the bag on a big plate, take it to the table and break open the foil. Feel free to vary the recipe – things like cooked new potatoes, a tablespoon of wholegrain mustard or a couple of handfuls of raw spinach are all good.

Sirloin of Beef with Pak Choy, Soy Sauce and Ginger

SERVES 2

2 x 225g/8oz sirloin steaks • sea salt and freshly ground
black pepper • 2 pak choy or bok choy (even spinach or any
other greens will do) • 8 tablespoons soy sauce • ½ a garlic
clove, finely grated • 1 thumb-sized piece of fresh ginger,
peeled and finely grated • 1 fresh chilli, deseeded and finely
grated • juice of 1 lime • 2 tablespoons olive oil

On a very hot griddle pan, cook your seasoned sirloin steaks until medium or to your liking. Place on a plate and allow to rest for 2 minutes, then cook your greens in salted boiling water until tender. While hot, douse the steaks with the soy sauce, and sprinkle with the garlic, ginger, chilli, lime juice and olive oil. When the greens are cooked, simply divide on to 2 plates, slice up the sirloin steaks, place on top of the greens and drizzle with any of the infused sauce left on the resting plate. A fantastic dish.

The Best Steak Sarnie

SERVES 2

1 ciabatta loaf or baguette • sea salt and freshly ground
black pepper • 1 x 285g/10oz rump steak •
2 sprigs of fresh rosemary, leaves picked • extra virgin olive oil
• juice of 1 lemon • 1–2 tablespoons Dijon mustard •
1 handful of rocket or watercress

Place your ciabatta just to warm in the oven for a few minutes at 100°C/225°F/
gas ¼. Season your steak and then sprinkle it with rosemary. Slice it across in half,
place the slices one at a time between 2 pieces of clingfilm, and bash with a flat
heavy object like a pot or cleaver or even your fist until 1cm/½ inch thick. Rub with
a little extra virgin olive oil, place on a very hot griddle or frying pan and sear each
side for a minute. This will cook the meat pink, but you can cook it less or more to
your liking. Remove to a plate, squeeze over the lemon juice and allow to rest while
you cut your ciabatta in half lengthways and drizzle the cut sides with a little extra
virgin olive oil. Smear a massive dollop of Dijon mustard over the bread, put your
steak and rocket on top, then drizzle over any juice from the meat. Squeeze together and eat!

Baked Cod with Avocado, Prawns, Cream and Cheese

SERVES 2

extra virgin olive oil • sea salt and freshly ground black
pepper • 2 x 225g/8oz cod fillets, skinned and pin-boned •
1 small handful of fresh basil, ripped • 1 avocado, peeled,
stoned, halved and sliced • 150g/5½oz good peeled prawns,
cooked or uncooked • 140ml/5fl oz double cream •
150g/5½oz good Cheddar cheese

Preheat the oven to 220°C/425°F/gas 7. Rub a baking dish or roasting tray with a
little olive oil, season the cod on both sides and place in the dish. Sprinkle the fillets with the basil, avocado and prawns. Drizzle over the cream and grate over the
cheese. Cook at the top of the preheated oven for 15–20 minutes until golden
brown and bubbling. Season to taste with sea salt and freshly ground black
pepper and serve simply with a green salad. Lovely jubbly.

Roasted Cod with Cherry Tomatoes, Basil and Mozzarella

SERVES 2

2 x 225g/8oz cod fillets, skinned and pin-boned • olive oil •
sea salt and freshly ground black pepper • 2 handfuls
of red and yellow cherry tomatoes, halved • 1 handful of fresh
basil, leaves picked • 1 ball of buffalo mozzarella, finely
sliced • 1 handful of grated Parmesan cheese

Preheat the oven to 220°C/425°F/gas 7. Place the cod fillets in an oiled roasting tray or an earthenware dish. Drizzle with olive oil and season. Place the tomatoes, basil and mozzarella on top of the fillets. Sprinkle over the Parmesan, drizzle over some olive oil, and bake at the top of the preheated oven for about 15–20 minutes, until golden.

Seared Salmon with Radicchio, Pancetta, Pinenuts and Balsamic Vinegar

SERVES 2

1 radicchio, halved through the core and sliced • 8 rashers of
pancetta or dry-cured smoked streaky bacon • 1 handful
of fresh marjoram or basil, leaves picked • 1 handful of
pinenuts, toasted • extra virgin olive oil • balsamic vinegar •
sea salt and freshly ground black pepper • 2 x 225g/8oz
salmon fillet steaks, skinned and pin-boned

Get a griddle pan very hot, then place your slices of radicchio on it. Char for around a minute on each side. Remove the radicchio and place in a bowl. Cook your pancetta or bacon on the griddle pan and then remove and add to the radicchio. Throw your marjoram and toasted pinenuts into the bowl and drizzle with 2 or 3 good lugs of extra virgin olive oil. Add 2 or 3 tablespoons of balsamic vinegar and season to taste. Sear off your salmon until just pink in the middle and serve with your radicchio and pancetta.

Salmon with Horseradish and Beets

SERVES 2

2 x 225g/8oz salmon fillets, pin-boned and scored ½cm
deep • salt and freshly ground black pepper • 6–8 baby
beetroots, cooked until tender then sliced • 1 small
handful of fresh marjoram, leaves picked • extra virgin
olive oil • balsamic vinegar • 2 tablespoons crème fraîche •
2 tablespoons creamed horseradish • juice of 1 lemon
• 1 handful of rocket or watercress

Add your salmon fillets, skin-side down, to a hot non-stick pan. Lightly press them with a spatula so they don't curl up. After a minute they should be lightly golden. Turn the salmon over, sprinkle with salt and then place under the grill for 10–15 minutes until just cooked. While cooking, marinate your beetroots with the marjoram, a little olive oil, balsamic vinegar and seasoning. Mix the crème fraîche with the horseradish and season to taste, carefully, with salt, pepper and lemon juice. Place the beets and salmon on your serving plates, sprinkle over the rocket and drizzle with the horseradish sauce.

HAVING A LAUGH

The title of this chapter may suggest otherwise, but it's really for parents. Getting your kids involved with food is definitely the way forward for cooking in this country. Shopping for the best ingredients then cooking and eating good-quality food with them is so important. Get your kids interested in all aspects of food – as well as being fun it can also be an education for them, which will stand them in good stead for later life. As I'm not a father (yet), this chapter is not inspired by being a father – it's much more about the kid I was when I first started cooking. About what caught my attention and fascinated me. Get your kids interested and you'll be on to a winner!

I now have friends with kids who really swear by getting them involved in the kitchen – I feel very strongly that parents have a responsibility to educate their kids not only to enjoy good food and understand it, but to take an interest in what they eat. This part of the book isn't about giving you ten or fifteen recipes and saying, 'Oh, and by the way these are for kids' – I think that's the wrong attitude. I'd like to think that kids can certainly get involved in some way in every single recipe in this book – obviously things like hot caramel, pans and sharp knives are no-nos for your bambinos, but there will always be little jobs that they can do.

Most importantly, cooking with your kids is not about making smiley faces on pizzas or baking hedgehog cookies and disguising food. It's about smelling, touching, creating, tasting, laughing and eating. I've got a handful of recipes in this chapter which are always a great laugh and success with the kids, but to be honest it's more about a vibe; capturing the attention and imagination of the young ones. I'd like to think it will encourage them to feel free to roam through the rest of the book, cooking anything they like with maybe a little help from their parents if need be.

THE TRADE-OFF

As always when it comes to kids, to begin with you will find yourself in a trade-off situation! When I was five, my mum, dad and all their chefs at the pub used to get me involved in cooking to keep me quiet for twenty minutes and to get some little jobs done. In return they would give me and my friends a big pile of ice-cream or push me on the rope swing for half an hour until I was sick – there was always a trade-off between me and them. You will soon find that trade-offs such as 'If you help me pod these peas, I'll make that favourite dessert of yours,' or 'If you don't help me I'll make you watch that Naked Chef on the TV,' will work wonders!

EDUCATION

Without sounding like a goody-goody or a preacher, in general kids' diets in Britain are a nightmare. Supermarkets, school dinners and cookery lessons should all try to help give families more knowledge about food. Just look at 90 per cent of kids' menus in restaurants – they're all the same: fish fingers, burgers, chicken nuggets and sausages. I'm not saying it's a bad thing and I know a lot of parents say, 'It's the only thing my little Joey will eat,' but some of the best experiences in my life, not only those involving food, have come through being forced to do or try different things. On a trip to Italy I saw a family with several small kids all tucking into grilled pigeon and gnawing the meat off the bones. They were also dipping crispy polenta into a spicy tomato sauce and loving it! It's terrific to see kids tucking in and enjoying tasty food without being worried about its colour, shape or texture. But also it's up to parents to make eating these types of foods a really exciting event. Try bigging up the more adventurous things by saying things like, 'Oh, isn't that lovely! Aren't you lucky, that'll put hairs on your chest' (cliché, cliché!). Good body language around food and kids also does the trick; smiles and coos of delight will all work. My mum and dad would encourage my sister and me to try things like crab and lobster with them – I didn't want to miss out on anything, so I tucked in.

SHOPPING

When I was as little as five years old, my dad used to take me to the fruit and veg market and to the cash and carry to get the essentials. I honestly used to feel slightly more grown-up and completely honoured when Dad used to say, 'Go on, son, I want you to go and pick me the best box of raspberries. Make sure you taste them, all right,' which I used to do with great concentration. He used to have me groping melons, eating apples and sniffing herbs. I would scurry back to Dad with my opinion and some for him to try. Then we'd negotiate a price together and put it all in the van to go back to the pub. Even though I loved it, I think my dad used to take liberties with me being too keen, as he would say, 'Listen to Dad and go and tell that man over there that his fruit and veg is too expensive and a load of old rubbish.' Which I did with great conviction − resulting in me legging it from the warehouse!

So really try to get the kids involved in making some shopping decisions, because all they want is to be treated like grown-ups. Instead of letting them trail behind you while you pile things into the trolley, ask them to choose a pineapple by smelling it to check that it's ripe, for instance. Kids are like sponges − they soak up information and remember everything − so talk to them, ask for their opinions on what fish looks good or what meat to try. This can be good fun, especially when you reach the deli counter, as you can try out different things with them. Ask your kids to taste Parma ham, then ask them what they think. No matter what, always let them have some input when out shopping and listen to them seriously. If they realize their opinion counts then they will want to get involved when it comes to cooking the ingredients.

CAPTURING THEIR IMAGINATION

As a kid I wasn't really that passionate about food, so it wasn't like I was born to cook. But living in a pub I did get to see a lot of preparation and different types of cooking from a young age, which was handy. Kids can get involved in all sorts of ways when it comes to cooking. There's so much more to learn from food than just eating it. I couldn't believe my eyes when I saw a piece of dough doubled in size and looking like The Blob! It was alive and I was absolutely mesmerized. How mad was that – something doubling in size over forty minutes. I was completely fascinated by the whole process: the proving, the shaping, the flavouring.

To Jamie Oliver

To   A poem for you.

Barbecuing on the beach
As the mewing seagulls screech,
The food your cooking
is yummy looking,
pucker tucker
who gets this supper,
friends of course, fiddling
while their mouths are dribbling
food looking so divine,
clever jamie serves on time
by Hannah Ridgment

A picture
in a shell

I saw you on the beach
but when I came to ask for your
autograph you had gone.

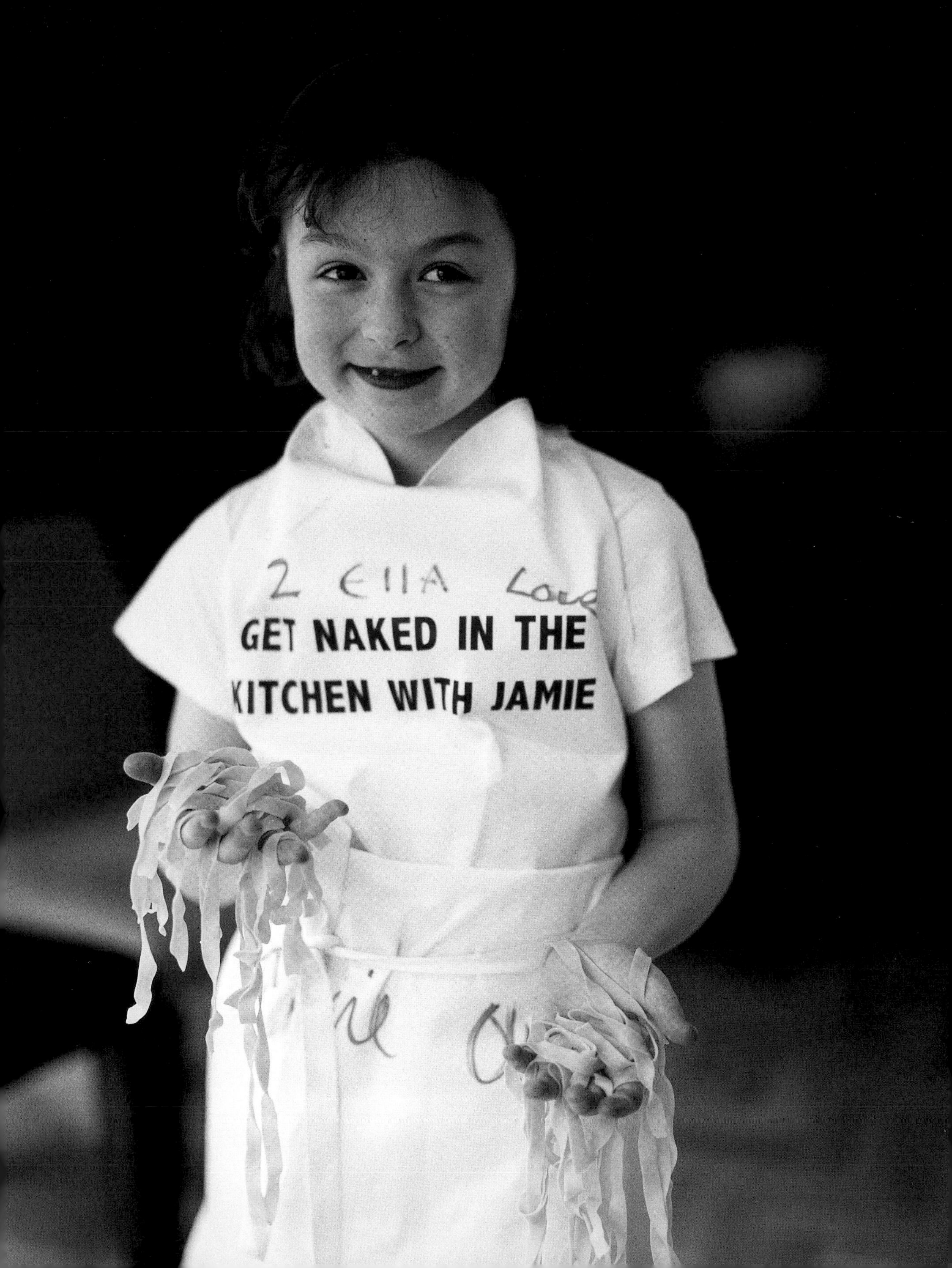
GET NAKED IN THE
KITCHEN WITH JAMIE

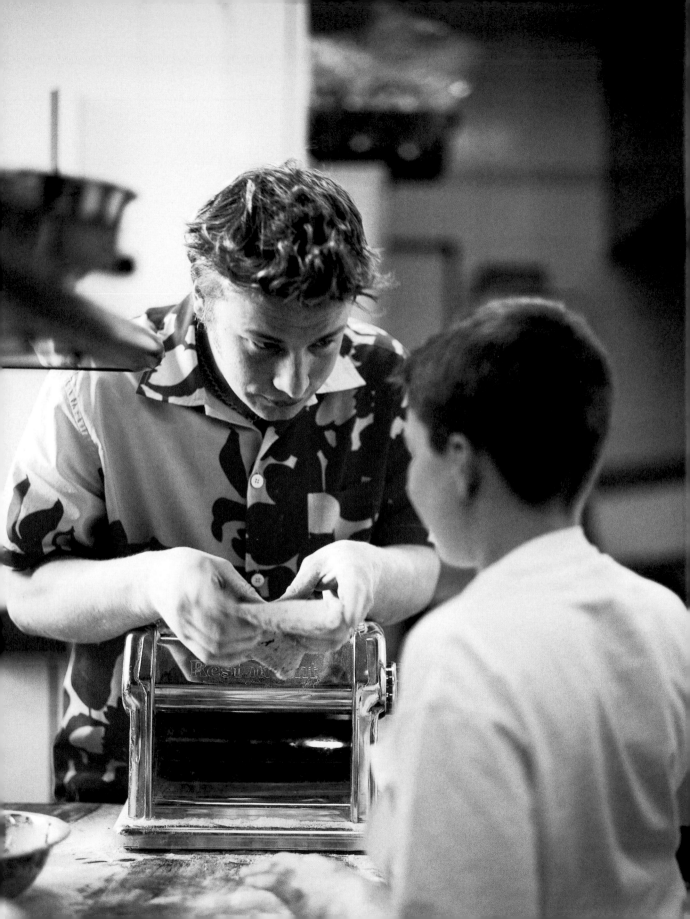

A CRAVING FOR COOKING

I craved responsibility as a kid. I wanted jobs to do; I wanted to muck in with every-one else. These days, I don't think enough responsibility for cooking is given to kids – maybe because parents are worried about them making a mess. It's so easy though; just teach them to make a great salad dressing in a jam jar – they can han-dle doing that. Then get them making the whole salad. And thank them for it – they'll want to do more. Some parents say, 'I'm going to cook with the kids today', and they just bake gingerbread men and stuff like that. This is great, but try to get them involved here and there all the time if you can. That's what it's all about. But remember, it's not about ramming it down their throats either, so find a balance to suit you. Kids should be able to make just about anything in this book, but watch out for things that involve excess heat, knives and machinery, plastic bags and clingfilm, which is not the end of the world because there is still a load of bashing, smashing, squeezing, stirring, tossing, drizzling and whipping to be done.

Here are some cooking ideas to try out with your kids:

Make marinades and bash spices in a pestle and mortar • Bash olives on a chopping board to remove the stones using one of their favourite mugs, like Thomas the Tank Engine, or something heavy; the stones should then be dropped into the mug – as sounds are so important in the kitchen, explain to your child that they should listen out for the stone hitting the mug • Pour oil over meat, fish or salads from a height • Pick herbs from the garden, smell them and rip them over a salad or finished pasta dish • Squeeze lemons • Squash tomatoes • Spin or toss salad leaves • Watch bread dough prove and check on it • Mash veg • And so much more ...

IT'S A FAMILY THING

When talking to adults who are passionate about food, you'll very often find that they'll reminisce about their mum in the kitchen. This shows how important parents are when we think of food. When I was growing up and we lived above the pub, we would have our dinner at half five every day. That was our time to sit down together as a family, which, looking back, was so important. It was a time for laughing and sharing. It's nice to get everyone around the table and turn the TV off (unless the World Cup is on, of course) and simply enjoy eating together.

Dried Fruitgums

A few of my friends feed their kids really nice dried apricots, plums, peaches, pineapple and apples as a treat instead of giving them boiled sugar sweets. Surprisingly the kids absolutely love them. I actually think that a little paper bag of dried fruit is quite cool, but my friends fool their bambinos by cutting the fruit into shapes to look more like sweets.

When I cook these 'fruitgums' I normally do about 500g or a kilo (1–2lb) of dried fruit at a time. You can do single types of fruit, or combos like mango and pineapple or peach and apricot. I simply whizz the dried fruit down to a very smooth purée in a Magimix food processor then scoop it out on to some greased greaseproof paper. Using a palette knife, spread it out into a square, about 0.5cm/¼ inch thick. Then slide this on to a baking tray. I normally heat the fruit purée in the electric oven at 70°C/150°F overnight, which is very convenient for me, or, if you're in a rush, heat it at 160°C/300°F/gas 2 for a couple of hours – the cooking time really depends on how moist the fruit was to start with.

When it's done, your layer of fruit should be soft but firm, a little bit like a winegum. Remove it from the oven to a chopping board, peel off the greaseproof paper and slice the fruit into small bite-sized pieces. Make a variety of shapes – squares, triangles, circles, strips. These can be kept in an airtight jar until you need them. It's lovely to wrap them in little paper bags and put them in your kids' lunchboxes. They'll love 'em.

Lolly Pops

My lovely nan and grandad used to run a village pub called the Plough and Sail in Paglesham in Essex. When I was a kid they used to send me and my sister, Anna-Marie, a huge box of about 200 ice lollies at the start of the summer holidays every year. The ice lollies would arrive with the deliveries from the same butcher that we've always shared and we would keep them in the big chest freezer outside in the store shed. This was great, as it meant I had a constant supply I could help myself to whenever I wanted. I was always quite popular with the local kids because of this. So much so that my supplies would dwindle very quickly. So, I started to make my own lolly pops.

The nice thing about them was that they weren't full of a thousand E numbers because I would make them out of apple juice, orange juice, lemonade, pineapple juice – all sorts of stuff. Even cocktail combinations are good. I would also sneak into the pub for some cider shandy to make lolly pops!

All you need to do to make lolly pops is buy a couple of those really cheap ice lolly sets. You can find them in most kitchen shops. Fill them up with your chosen juice and put the stick in before freezing. It's nice to have something cold and fruity to hand in your freezer when it's a scorcher outside.

Smush Ins

Smush ins are one of the coolest things to make (see pages 62–3). I remember when I was a kid, me and my sister would always try to defrost our hard ice-cream in our dessert bowls into almost a thick milkshakey consistency before scoffing the lot. Then as we matured we realized that many flavours could be mushed in to improve the flavour of the rubbishy ice-cream that our parents always used to give us.

So, from the word 'mush' and the phrase 'mushing it in' they became 'smush ins'. It was great going round the supermarkets as a kid secretly slipping possible smush ins into the trolley. Anything could be a contender – from maple syrup to bashed up chocolate bits, meringue, fruit – you name it, we would smush it! Winegums aren't so good though. But melted chocolate caramel bars are chooooooice.

All you need to do is get a big pot of vanilla ice-cream and a selection of possible smush ins (see the picture on the next page for inspiration). Take 2 large scoops of ice-cream per person, blob these on to a clean chopping board, sprinkle or dribble over your flavours and then, with a spatula or fork, mush and smush them together. Scoop up and lob into a bowl or cornet.

Give these a bash and make an event of them when you've got all the kids round. They're really good fun and great to use as bribes to get the kids helping you with the proper cooking! Smush away.

Chocolate Biscuits with Soft Chocolate Centres

This is a great recipe to do with kids, as it's very simple and good fun putting the top circle over the chocolate and squashing the edges gently together to stop the chocolate escaping when it cooks. This is quite a dry mixture, but don't worry, they are meant to look a bit cracked and rustic, so you can't really go wrong! If you eat these when they have just been cooked the chocolate is quite runny, and if you eat them cold they are nice and gooey. You'll need two cutters, one about 4cm/1½ inches and the other about 5cm/2 inches.

MAKES 30 BISCUITS

140g/5oz butter • 140g/5oz caster sugar • 2 egg yolks • 255g/9oz self-raising flour • 30g/1oz cocoa powder • 30 squares of chocolate (milk, white or plain)

Grease a large baking sheet. Cream the butter and sugar together until pale. Beat in the egg yolks, then add the flour and cocoa powder to make a dough. Turn out and knead, then pop it into the fridge for a while. Preheat the oven to 190°C/375°F/gas 5.

On a lightly floured surface, roll about a third of the dough out thinly, then cut out about 30 circles with the smaller cutter (you can do fewer if you want the biscuits bigger). Spread them out on the baking sheet and put a square of the chocolate in the middle of each one – make sure you use all of the chocolate however many you do. Then roll the rest of the dough out (I always add the leftovers from the first lot of cutting to it and knead it a bit). Cut out the same number of circles with the larger cutter and pop them on top of the chocolate, pressing gently all the way round to seal the edge and keep all the chocolate in.

Cook in the preheated oven for 10 minutes, and eat them hot or cold.

Sticky Toffee Cupcakes with Chocolate Topping

Whatever happened to cupcakes? I used to love them as a kid and, while mucking about with a sticky toffee pudding recipe, I tried to reinvent the good old cupcake — always puts a smile on my face.

MAKES ABOUT 12

30g/1oz sultanas • 30g/1oz dried apricots • 30g/1oz dates •
1 teaspoon baking powder • 140g/5oz self-raising flour •
30g/1oz muscovado sugar • 1 tablespoon golden syrup •
1 large egg • 30g/1oz melted butter • 140ml/5fl oz hot water

FOR THE CHOCOLATE TOPPING

40g/1½oz butter • 40g/1½oz caster sugar • 40g/1½oz plain chocolate • 70ml/2½fl oz double cream

Preheat the oven to 200°C/400°F/gas 6. In a food processor, blitz the sultanas, apricots, dates, baking powder and a little of the flour (just enough to stop the fruit sticking to the blades). If you don't have a food processor, you can chop it very finely. Put this mixture into a bowl with the muscovado sugar, the golden syrup, the egg and the melted butter and stir together. Then add the very hot water and the remaining flour and mix well with a whisk. Divide the mixture between 12 cupcake papers (I like to double up the papers to give the mixture a bit more hold) and place on a baking tray. Bake in the preheated oven for about 15 minutes.

Meanwhile, melt all the chocolate topping ingredients in a saucepan and bubble for a while until darkened in colour slightly. Remove from the heat and let the sauce cool until it thickens. Then put a blob on top of each cupcake.

Frozen Yoghurt

This is almost like ice-cream, can be any flavour you like, and is really tasty and refreshing, but more importantly it's so, so quick to make as you don't have to do any whipping or freezing. Just a bit of help from your trusty Magimix and some frozen fruit.

SERVES 4–6

310g/11oz good frozen fruit (strawberries, raspberries, blueberries, etc.) • 1 x 500g/1lb 2oz tub of live yoghurt • 2 tablespoons good honey • optional: cornets or wafers

The only important thing to remember here is that your fruit should be in the freezer and frozen and your yoghurt in the fridge and cold before you start. Remove the fruit and place it in your food processor. Blitz for 30 seconds, add the yoghurt and honey, and blend for a minute until smooth. At this point, taste for sweetness – fruit is normally frozen when it's ripe and at its best, so it should be pretty perfect. If not, add some more honey. It should be scoopable, so eat it straight away or put it into a covered bowl and place in the freezer, where it will keep for a couple of weeks. How good is that?

MORE SIMPLE SALADS You'd think there wouldn't be any more salads, or at least any half-decent classy salads left to talk about – but no, we are back with a vengeance. My addiction to the crisp leaf has given me some fantastic ideas which I know you will love. Salads are always great for snacks, lunch or dinner. I've even been known to come back from band practice at two in the morning and do a nice crispy bacon, rocket and Parmesan salad with a bit of balsamic dressing. Not quite a Ruby Murray, but still scrumptious none the less. I have also included six fantastic dressings which I know people love – good dressings make good salads even out of a dodgy bit of iceberg lettuce which tastes of nothing.

I've got a mate called Andy Slade, the local gasman back in Essex, who swears, as a bachelor just moved into his new house, that 'I eat helffy now, Ollie.' I say, 'What do you mean, Andy?' as I look round his kitchen, noticing the plugs and manuals are still in their plastic wrappers inside the oven and washing machine. He replies, 'Well, I always order extra salad in my doner kebab.' What can I say? He needs help … or the love, sympathy and bravery of a good woman!

Andy the gasman

Ollie

Marinated Mozzarella in Crème Fraîche with Lemon and Marjoram

I always love making this salad because it transforms a piece of lovely mozzarella cheese into something really special. In fact, it's classy enough to be a nice starter with a little chopped fresh tomato on some grilled bruschetta.

Simply slice up 4 balls of buffalo mozzarella around 1 cm/½ inch thick, place on a large plate or dish and smear over a small tub or 6 heaped tablespoons of crème fraîche. Season with sea salt and freshly ground black pepper to taste. Wash and peel 1 lemon with a vegetable peeler and finely chop half of the rind. Sprinkle this over the mozzarella and créme fraîche and squeeze over half the juice. Put the left-over lemon to one side in case the flavour needs tweaking later. Sprinkle over a good handful of fresh marjoram leaves. Taste once more for a good balance of flavour.

Halve, deseed and finely slice a couple of fresh chillies. Sprinkle them over your mozzarella, drizzle over 4 tablespoons of extra virgin olive oil, and serve in the middle of the table or as part of another dish. Any leftovers will keep for a couple of days in the fridge and are just as scrumptious on a piece of cod baked in the oven – you must try it.

The Easiest Sexiest Salad in the World

SERVES 4

I love this salad. Apart from being a great combination, it always seems unbelievably effortless, which is the kind of recipe I like. The constant success of this is due to the common-sense marriage of salty Parma ham, milky buffalo mozzarella and sweet figs, which obviously need to be of a good quality. The best figs to use are Italian and the best time to buy them is June to August when they are in season. Greek figs are a good second-best and are in season from September to November. The best figs always seem to be those that are about to split their skins. Use green or black figs – it doesn't really matter.

One thing I do is to criss-cross the figs but not quite to the bottom – 1 fig per person is always a good start. Then, using your thumbs and forefingers, squeeze the base of the fig to expose the inside. At this point you'll think, 'Oooh, that looks nice, I think I'm quite clever...' or at least I do. More importantly, it allows your dressing to get right into the middle of the fig. All these little things really help to make a salad special. Simply place the figs in a dish, weave around 1 slice of Parma ham or prosciutto per fig, throw in some slices of buffalo mozzarella, rip over some green or purple basil and drizzle everything with the honey and lemon juice dressing (page 115). As far as salads go, it's pretty damn sexy.

PS It's a good idea to have some spare bread on the table to mop up the juices – always a treat.

Courgette Salad with Mint, Garlic, Red Chilli, Lemon and Extra Virgin Olive Oil

SERVES 4

This is quite an unusual salad and terribly simple to make. It's great because it's a nice little side dish that will go with things like mozzarella, goat's cheese, cured meats, grilled or barbecued white fish like cod or haddock, even things like chicken or pork. Use courgettes when at their best (nice and firm and not too big).

Slice 4 courgettes lengthways as thin as you can (use a mandolin if you have one). Grill on a red-hot griddle pan, or on the barbecue, until lightly charred on each side. Scatter the slices over a large plate, making sure you don't sit them on top of each other otherwise they'll steam and go a bit limp, and there's nothing worse than limp courgettes, I can tell you. While they're still warmish, sprinkle them with a little sea salt and freshly ground black pepper.

Deseed a red chilli and chop finely. Finely chop ½ a clove of garlic and sprinkle the chilli and garlic evenly from a height over the courgettes. (Add to your own taste, but just remember that when the chilli and garlic mix with the olive oil and lemon juice the heat and flavours are lessened.)

Tear over a handful of fresh mint and drizzle with good extra virgin olive oil and a squeeze of lemon. I've even been known to throw in some blanched broad beans or raw peas if I can get any. This salad is always a real treat.

PS If you find yourself with leftovers, try baking any fish fillets (cod, haddock or bass for example) on top of the courgettes. Lovely with steamed rice and seasoned yoghurt. Very fresh and good for you.

Japanese Cucumber Salad with Ginger, Coriander, Mint and Rice Wine Vinegar Dressing

In our supermarkets we have been blessed with a new type of cucumber which is about a third of the size of normal cucumbers. I really like them because they are a touch firmer and ideal for this oriental salad. Wash 3 cucumbers and finely slice along their length with a mandolin or one of those cheap old potato peelers. Basically you want to get very fine strips of cucumber. Place the strips on a plate and spread them out. Sprinkle with some ripped-up fresh mint and coriander and drizzle generously with the ginger and rice wine vinegar dressing (page 115).

Scrummy Warm Rocket Salad

SERVES 4

Warm salads can be blooming amazing or a complete disaster. First, you have got to get your hungry guests around the table before you plate up, so as soon as their bums are on the chairs, you are tossing the warm ingredients in with the rocket leaves. Boom, boom, boom on a plate and it's in front of them.

Peel, halve and quarter 2 medium red onions, then quarter again, to give you 8 pieces from each onion. Heat a frying pan and fry off 8 whole rashers of pancetta or smoked streaky bacon until crisp. Remove, add a couple of lugs of olive oil to the pan, and add 4 sprigs of thyme, the onions and a good handful of pinenuts with a pinch of salt. Toss around and fry on a medium heat for about 5 minutes until caramelized and sweet (not black!). Put your pancetta or bacon back into the pan, toss around, then throw everything into a salad bowl with 4 big handfuls of rocket or any nice salad leaves. Drizzle generously with balsamic vinegar – this will make a natural dressing as it mixes with the olive oil. Serve with some shaved Parmesan over the top – you can use a potato peeler to do this. Munch away.

Japanese Mooli Salad with Mustard Cress, Crème Fraîche and Grilled Lemon Dressing

SERVES 4–6

This salad uses fantastic Japanese moolis, which are kind of like oriental radishes. They are crunchy and slightly mustardy in taste and now widely available.

Peel one of these boys and thinly slice it lengthways with a potato peeler or a mandolin. Once that's done, take 4 or 5 of the slices at a time, line them up together on a chopping board and run your knife down the length of them, cutting them into strips rather like tagliatelle – don't be fussy about getting them exactly the same size. Cutting them into thin strips will help your dressing to stick to the mooli, making it taste lovely jubbly.

Mix the mooli strips in a bowl with 3 punnets of mustard cress, tops trimmed, earthy parts binned. Dress with the crème fraîche and grilled lemon dressing (page 114) and season well to taste. Just to get you thinking, in Japan they slice up fine slivers of mango, raw red mullet and scallops into this salad, which I love – the dressing slightly cures the fish, giving it a nice chewy richness which is great. Give it a bash.

Avocado, Spring Onion, Coriander and Chilli Salad
with Toasted Almonds

SERVES 4

Nothing very worldly to say about this salad except it's very tasty. I had a flash of inspiration when looking at my slightly bare fridge and came up with this. It's rather nice with some cold roast chicken, especially in a bit of pitta bread.

Throw a couple of good handfuls of whole blanched almonds into a non-stick pan with the smallest amount of olive oil and toast until lightly golden in the oven, under the grill or over the gas. Whichever way you choose, keep your eyes peeled so they don't burn. Season with salt, pepper and a little dried red chilli and put to one side. You will want 3 or 4 avocados, halved, peeled and with the stone removed. Tear the avocado into chunky bits, place in a bowl, sprinkle over 4 or 5 finely sliced spring onions and as much finely sliced fresh green chilli as you like, and rip over a handful of coriander. Then sprinkle over the almonds, drizzle with plenty of thick mustard dressing (page 114) and season with salt and pepper.

A Tuscan Raw Artichoke, Rocket and Parmesan Salad

SERVES 4

When globe artichokes come into season it's always a real treat in Tuscany to be given a bowl of this salad. To prepare the salad, you need one globe artichoke per person. See pages 218–19 for preparation instructions and pictures. Rub the trimmed artichokes with a little lemon to stop them discolouring. Simply slice very finely, then give them a good squeeze of lemon, some extra virgin olive oil, salt and pepper to taste and a big handful of rocket. Toss everything together in a bowl and shave over lots of Parmesan cheese, using a vegetable peeler or a knife. I love eating this salad on its own before dinner. Raw artichokes are very good for you.

Globe Artichoke, Pink Grapefruit, Frisée and Pecorino Salad

SERVES 4

For this recipe you could buy good preserved artichokes to save time. If using fresh, whack 8 nice globe artichokes into a large pot of salted water, bring to the boil and cook for around 15 minutes (time will depend on their size), until a small knife slides easily into the base. Drain in a colander under running water for a couple of minutes and allow to cool while you segment 2 grapefruits, keeping the juice (see below). Place the segments and any juice in a bowl with a handful of golden, toasted almonds. Peel off the outer green leaves of your artichokes until you reach the soft and tender yellow ones. With a sharp knife trim off the top and bottom of the artichoke, leaving you with the tender heart. Slice in half and then remove the choke from the middle using a teaspoon. Add the artichokes to the grapefruit and almonds. Drizzle with the honey and lemon juice dressing (page 115). Add 3 large handfuls of frisée, then toss together. Shave over some pecorino cheese, using a vegetable peeler, and serve immediately.

Warm Bread Salad of Crispy Pancetta, Parmesan and Poached Egg

SERVES 4

1 ciabatta loaf • extra virgin olive oil • 1 clove of garlic, peeled
and sliced • sea salt and freshly ground black pepper •
12 slices of pancetta or dry-cured smoked streaky bacon • juice
of 1 lemon • 4 large organic eggs (must be very fresh) •
3 large handfuls of rocket • 1 oak leaf lettuce • 100g/3½ oz
Parmesan cheese, in one piece

Preheat the oven to 200°C/400°F/gas 6. Remove the crusts from the ciabatta and discard, then tear the bread into finger-sized pieces. Place on a baking tray, drizzle with a little olive oil and toss with the garlic and seasoning. Bake for 10 minutes until crisp, then lay the pancetta over the bread and bake for 5 more minutes until that's crispy too. Mix the lemon juice with 8 tablespoons of oil and season. Put a big pan of unsalted water on to boil.

In a large bowl toss the salad leaves, pancetta, bread and dressing together, then divide between 4 plates. When the pan of water is simmering, add your 4 eggs. They must be really fresh for successful poached eggs. Cook for 4 minutes for a soft egg, or to your liking. Place an egg on each salad and shave over your Parmesan, using a vegetable peeler. Sweeeet!!!

The Best Pasta Salad

SERVES 4

310g/11oz small shell-shaped pasta • 3 cloves of garlic
• 255g/9oz yellow cherry tomatoes • 255g/9oz red
cherry tomatoes • 1 handful of black olives, pitted •
2 tablespoons fresh chives • 1 handful of fresh basil •
½ a cucumber • 4 tablespoons white wine vinegar, or to
taste • 7 tablespoons extra virgin olive oil • sea salt
and freshly ground black pepper

Bring a large pan of salted water to the boil. Throw in the pasta and cloves of garlic, boil until al dente, drain and run under cold water to cool. Put the garlic to one side to use for the dressing. Put the pasta into a bowl. Chop the tomatoes, olives, chives, basil and cucumber into pieces about half the size of the pasta and add to the bowl. Squash the garlic cloves out of their skins and mush in a pestle and mortar. Add the vinegar, oil and seasoning. Drizzle this over the salad, adding a little more seasoning to taste.

dress

sing

Herb Vinegar and Roasted Garlic Dressing

3 cloves of garlic, unpeeled and roasted or boiled until soft
• 6 tablespoons olive oil • 1 heaped teaspoon Dijon
mustard • 3 tablespoons good herb vinegar, red or white •
sea salt and freshly ground black pepper

Squeeze garlic out of its skin, mush up and mix in a bowl with the
other ingredients.

Crème Fraîche and Grilled Lemon Dressing

1 large lemon, halved • 3 tablespoons olive oil •
3 tablespoons crème fraîche or mayonnaise • 2 heaped
teaspoons Dijon mustard • sea salt, freshly ground
black pepper and soy sauce

Grill your lemon halves on a griddle pan for 5 minutes until soft and
charred. Squeeze the juice into a bowl. Add the rest of the ingredients,
mix together and season to taste.

Thick Mustard Dressing

6 tablespoons extra virgin olive oil • 2 heaped tablespoons
Dijon mustard • 1 heaped tablespoon wholegrain
mustard • 2 tablespoons white wine vinegar • sea salt and
freshly ground black pepper

Mix everything together in a bowl and season to taste.

Honey and Lemon Juice Dressing

6 tablespoons extra virgin olive oil • 3 tablespoons
lemon juice • 1 tablespoon good honey • sea salt and
freshly ground black pepper

Mix everything together in a bowl and season to taste.

Ginger and Rice Wine Vinegar Dressing

6 tablespoons olive oil • 3 tablespoons rice wine vinegar •
1 teaspoon sugar • 1 large thumb-sized piece of ginger, peeled
and finely grated • 1 stick of lemon grass, outer leaves
removed, inner ones finely chopped • sea salt,
freshly ground black pepper and soy sauce

Mix everything together in a bowl and season to taste.

Bashed-up Pinenut, Basil and Balsamic Dressing

½ a clove of garlic, peeled and bashed to a pulp • 1 good
handful of fresh basil, bashed to a pulp • 1 small
handful of toasted pinenuts, bashed to bits • 6 tablespoons
olive oil • 3 tablespoons balsamic vinegar • sea salt
and freshly ground black pepper

Mix everything together in a bowl and season to taste.

Gennaro

Curly

Mauro

PASTA No matter what I do, where I go or who I meet, pasta always comes through with flying colours as one of my favourite regular meals. So I've put together some superb little pasta dishes which will see you through from comfort food to dinner parties. This time I've used mostly dried pasta, as it's so convenient and cheap. Don't be fooled into thinking that fresh pasta is the best – it's just different. Fresh pasta lends itself better to creamy, buttery sauces, while dried pasta is better with tomato- and olive oil-based sauces. If, however, you do fancy making fresh pasta, then take a look at my other two books.

Spaghetti with Sweet Cherry Tomatoes, Marjoram and Extra Virgin Olive Oil

When tomatoes are good, this is super nice. It's a warm dish as opposed to hot, but is even great when cold as a salad for picnics.

SERVES 4

455g/1lb dried spaghetti, spaghettini or linguine •
310–400g/11–14oz ripe cherry tomatoes, red and yellow •
2 good handfuls of fresh marjoram or basil, leaves
picked • 6–8 lugs extra virgin olive oil • 1 clove of garlic,
peeled and finely sliced • 1 tablespoon white or red wine
vinegar • sea salt and freshly ground black pepper

Put your pasta into a large pan of salted boiling water and cook until al dente (check the packet for cooking time). While it's cooking, halve the tomatoes, put them into a large bowl, and add your herbs, olive oil, garlic and vinegar. Season to taste, and scrunch with your hands to slightly mush the tomatoes. This can sit now until the pasta's ready. Drain the pasta, and while still steaming hot mix well with the tomatoes, check the seasoning and serve. Easy peasy.

Spaghetti with Salami, Fennel and Tomatoes

SERVES 4

extra virgin olive oil • 140g/5oz good spicy Italian salami, sliced • 2 cloves of garlic, peeled and finely sliced • 1 teaspoon fennel seeds • 1 bulb of fennel, halved and finely sliced, feathery tops reserved and chopped • 2 x 400g/14oz tins of plum tomatoes • optional: 1 dried chilli, crumbled • sea salt and freshly ground black pepper • 455g/1lb dried spaghetti or linguine • 2 handfuls of stale breadcrumbs • optional: a sprig of fresh rosemary

Pour 2 good lugs of olive oil into a pan. Add your salami and your sliced garlic. Lightly crack the fennel seeds either in a pestle and mortar or with a knife and add to the pan. Cook for 1 minute on a low heat – the fat should cook out of the salami and it should begin to get crisp. Add your sliced fennel and stir, then put the lid on the pan and increase the heat to medium. Cook for 5 minutes, then add your tinned tomatoes and even a little dried chilli if you like. Cook slowly for 25 minutes until the mixture has thickened. Season to taste.

Cook your pasta in a large pot of fast-boiling salted water until al dente (check the packet for cooking time). While it's cooking I like to make pangritata (crunchy breadcrumbs), to give this dish a great texture and crunch. Just get a couple of good handfuls of coarse breadcrumbs – I do this by removing the crusts from some stale bread and whizzing them up until kind of coarse in a Magimix food processor. Fry the crumbs with 4 or 5 tablespoons of extra virgin olive oil until they go crispy. Sometimes I throw in some rosemary sprigs as well to give extra flavour. When your pasta is cooked, drain it in a colander and immediately toss it with your lovely tomato sauce. This is quite rich but very very tasty.

Serve in a large bowl and sprinkle with the green fennel tops and your crispy golden pangritata. Eat immediately, with a good glass of red wine.

PS I've eaten a couple of pasta dishes similar to this in Tuscany. Sometimes really good sausages or sliced, cured salamis are used. It's quite a blokey, hearty pasta but the fennel does cut through and make it a little fresher and more delicate.

Kinda Spaghetti Bolognaise

As far as I know, no decent Italian cook has any real recollection of what we know as Spaghetti Bolognaise. However, every region in Italy makes its own ragú sauce which very often features leftover stewed meats and game. For a great bolognaise it's worth whizzing up some chopped chuck steak to make your own minced meat. Here's my version.

SERVES 4

10 slices of pancetta or smoked streaky bacon rashers, sliced • 1 handful of rosemary, leaves picked and roughly chopped • olive oil • 1 large onion, finely chopped • 3 cloves of garlic, finely chopped • 455g/1lb chuck steak, minced, or best minced beef • 1 wineglass of red wine • 1 level teaspoon dried oregano • 1 x 400g/14oz tin of tomatoes • 1 x 200g/7oz tube tomato purée or 1 small jar of sun-dried tomatoes, finely chopped • sea salt and freshly ground black pepper • 455g/1lb dried spaghetti • 1 handful of fresh basil • 2 handfuls of grated Parmesan or strong Cheddar cheese

Preheat the oven to 180°C/350°F/gas 4. In a large hot pan that can go in the oven, fry the pancetta and rosemary in a little olive oil until lightly golden. Then add the onion and garlic and fry for a further 3 minutes, until softened, before adding the minced beef. Stir and continue frying for 2 or 3 minutes before adding the wine. Reduce slightly, then add the oregano, all the tomatoes, and the tomato purée. Season well to taste, bring to the boil, cover with greaseproof paper or a lid, and place in the preheated oven for an hour and a half. Towards the end of the cooking time, put your spaghetti into a large pot of fast-boiling salted water until al dente (check the packet for cooking time). When it's cooked, drain it in a colander.

Just before serving, add some ripped-up fresh basil to the sauce. Serve with your spaghetti and some grated Parmesan or strong Cheddar. A green salad is also nice with this.

Honeymoon Spaghetti

I first tried this at Hotel St Pietro in Positano, Italy, where Jools and I stayed for a week of our honeymoon. You will need a piece of baking parchment measuring 60 x 120cm/2 x 4ft to make a large cooking parcel. The steam will cause the 'parcel' to puff up in the oven, which looks good at the table if you serve it straight away. My dad hasn't stopped cooking it – maybe he's got a second wind – the little tiger!

SERVES 4

1 x 1.5kg/3½lb crab or lobster • 2 cloves of garlic, chopped • 1 fresh red chilli, deseeded and finely sliced • 30g/1oz butter • 1 tablespoon olive oil • 455g/1lb live mussels, cleaned • 115g/4oz squid, sliced • 170g/6oz shelled tiger or small prawns • 455g/1lb spaghetti, cooked al dente • 1 handful of flat-leaf parsley and marjoram, roughly chopped • 1 egg, beaten

FOR THE SAUCE

1 tablespoon olive oil • 3 cloves of garlic, roughly chopped • 1 fresh red chilli, finely chopped • 2 x 400g/14oz tins of plum tomatoes • sea salt and freshly ground black pepper

Preheat the oven to 180°C/350°F/gas 4. Plunge the crab or lobster into boiling water, boil for 15 minutes, then remove. When cooled, remove all the meat from the shell, flaking it up into small pieces, and removing any splinters of shell.

To make the sauce, fry the empty shell and legs in the olive oil with the garlic and chilli. Using the end of a rolling pin, pound up the shells. Add the tomatoes and a large glass of water and simmer for 1 hour. Pass through a sieve, season to taste and put aside.

In a large pan gently fry the garlic and chilli from the main ingredients list in the butter and olive oil. Turn the heat up and add the mussels, squid and prawns. Cook for 2 minutes. Remove from the heat, discarding any unopened mussels. Add the tomato sauce, cooked spaghetti, lobster or crab meat and herbs and mix together.

Fold the parchment in half to get a crease and open it out again. Place the seafood mixture in the centre of one half and brush all the edges with egg. Bring the two sides together and seal well. Carefully slide the parcel on to a baking tray and cook for about 10 minutes until puffed up. Serve straight away.

Classic Penne Carbonara

This is the way it should be done, guys. Simple, quick and cheap – happy days.

SERVES 4

455g/1lb dried penne • 10 slices of pancetta or dry-cured
smoky bacon • olive oil • 5 organic egg yolks •
100ml/3½fl oz double cream • 125g/4½oz Parmesan cheese,
grated • salt and freshly ground black pepper

Cook the penne in salted boiling water until al dente (check the packet for cook-ing time). While the pasta's cooking, slowly fry the pancetta in a little oil until crispy. Break it up a bit, then put to one side. In a bowl, whip up the egg yolks, cream and half the Parmesan. When the pasta is cooked, drain it and immediately toss it with the warm, crispy pancetta and the egg mixture. A lot of carbonaras are over-cooked and resemble a scrambled egg sauce – if you add the penne immediately the residual heat is enough to cook the eggs and for the sauce to stay smooth and silky. Season well, using plenty of freshly ground black pepper, and add extra Parmesan to taste. Serve straight away, with a big bowl of salad and a nice bottle of red wine.

Open Lasagne of Sweet Tomatoes, Squid, Mussels, Farro and Olives

This dish is a real joy, inspired by a great American chef called Mario Bartelli who made me a simple squid stew on one of my trips to America. He called it 'two-minute squid' and it has stayed in my memory ever since. I've changed it slightly so that it is now a pukka pasta dish, but it can be thinned slightly with a little stock to make a great soup, or you can use it as a sauce over some grilled fish. Tossed with lasagne, like this, or with some tagliatelle, it's brilliant. Farro is a grain, similar to couscous or bulghur wheat, which has a great nutty flavour.

SERVES 6

1 red onion, finely chopped • 2 cloves of garlic, finely sliced • 55g/2oz farro • 2 handfuls of black olives, stones left in • 2 x 400g/14oz tins of tomatoes • 400g/14oz mussels, cleaned • 400g/14oz clams, cleaned • 310g/11oz squid, cleaned, trimmed and sliced • 12 sheets of fresh lasagne • sea salt and freshly ground black pepper • 1 handful of fresh parsley, chopped • extra virgin olive oil

In a large pot, slowly fry the onion and garlic in a little olive oil for 1 minute, then add the farro, olives and tomatoes and simmer for 30 minutes. Add the mussels and clams to the pot and shake around until they all open up (discard any that remain closed). Then add the squid and simmer for 1 minute. Remove the meat from most of the shells, then put your pasta on to cook until al dente in boiling salted water (check the packet for cooking time). Season the sauce carefully, throw in the parsley, and add 5 tablespoons of extra virgin olive oil to give it a good shine. When the pasta is cooked, toss with the sauce and serve immediately.

Parsnip and Pancetta Tagliatelle with Parmesan and Butter

I'd never thought of the parsnip and pancetta combination until about a year ago – slightly unusual, but what a great combo. It's bloody good and I've used them together ever since in soups, risottos, roasts and casseroles.

SERVES 4

12 slices of pancetta or dry-cured smoked streaky bacon • 1 handful of fresh rosemary, thyme or summer savory, leaves picked • 4 good knobs of butter • 2 cloves of garlic, peeled and finely sliced • 2 parsnips, peeled, halved and finely sliced lengthways • 455g/1lb dried tagliatelle • 3 good handfuls of grated Parmesan cheese • sea salt and freshly ground black pepper

In a large, non-stick frying pan fry your pancetta and herbs in half the butter for 2 minutes, then add the garlic and parsnips. Cook for a further 3 minutes on a medium heat, until the pancetta is slightly golden and the parsnips have softened nicely. Cook your tagliatelle in salted boiling water (check the packet for cooking time), then drain, reserving a little of the cooking water. Mix the pasta with the parsnips and pancetta and stir in the rest of your butter and the Parmesan, adding a little of the cooking water to loosen the mixture and make it creamy and shiny. Season to taste.

Broccoli and Anchovy Orecchiette

You must try this one. Penne and rigatoni are fine in place of orecchiette – and widely available everywhere.

SERVES 4

2 large heads of broccoli • 2 large cloves of garlic, peeled and chopped • 8 anchovy fillets • 2–4 small dried red chillies, crumbled, to your taste • 4 good knobs of butter • 455g/1lb dried orecchiette • sea salt and freshly ground black pepper • 2 good handfuls of grated Parmesan cheese, to taste

Using a small knife, trim round the broccoli to remove the dark green flowers from the main stalks and put them to one side. Peel the stalk, trim off the dry end and throw this away. Finely chop the stalk and put into a large pan with the garlic, anchovies, chillies and half the butter. Cover with a lid and cook slowly for 8–10 minutes while you cook your pasta in salted boiling water. This should take about the same length of time – check the packet. Something I like to do which is slightly different (but better, I'd like to think) is to cook the broccoli flowers with the pasta for the last 4 minutes – this makes them soft enough to eat but leaves them with great colour and texture.

   Drain the pasta and broccoli, saving a little of the cooking water, then toss into the other pan. Remove the pan from the heat. Season to taste with salt, pepper, the rest of the butter and a large handful of Parmesan. Mix well, adding a little of the cooking water if necessary to loosen the pasta and make it shine. Serve immediately, sprinkled with the rest of the Parmesan.

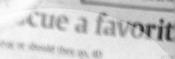

...cue a favorit

Here 'Rosie' maga...

O'Donnell s... revamp of '... celebrates h...

By Ann Oldenburg and Jean...
USA TODAY

With a look taken fro... Living, but with the size an... Rosie O'Donnell's new mag... newsstands Tuesday.

Less glossy, more crafty. The... masthead as editorial director... tress Fran Drescher for the co... Inside are stories on beauty... cooking, crafts, real people and... a personal piece on gun contro...

rosie

Oprah Winfrey's and Martha Stew... "Martha set the standards for wide-co... Oprah copied that, and I copied it as...

The star gives full credit to Winfrey... O'Donnell was asked to do a magazi... 'How could I? What would I do?"...

When O came out last year, "It was, '... take your show and put it in magazine... the essence and feeling of what you give... ers on a daily basis.'"

At first, she says, it wasn't easy worki... editorial staff. "My ideas shocked the... laughed at many of her suggestions, and sa... print that." One was a quiz with a joke li... heroin habit. They didn't want the "comedy... that is a spoof of the *O* and *Martha* calen... made it in. She wanted model Iman, wed... Bowie, for a cover, to tell about her amazing... the most intelligent woman I ever met in... ness." Editors seem...

Show time: Jamie Oliver, 25, has an energy that has made him a TV star and a hot cookbook author.

By Alastair Grant for USA TODAY

Brit's a rock star in chef's clothing

TV's 'Naked' sensation ser...
books...

SOMETHING FISHY GOING ON Fish is a fantastic thing. When you look at the way the Spanish, Italians and Japanese live and at their statistics of life expectancy, their consumption of fish seems to play a large part. I don't think any doctor has ever ruled out the fact that fish is really really good for your diet. So if you are a grumpy bugger, or you're married to one, who will only eat fish in batter, hopefully this chapter will be enough to twist your arm. Not only does fresh fish need minimal cooking, but it's damn tasty too. Think of your tastebuds, think of your heart and do yourself a favour – eat fresh fish at least twice a week. When buying fish you should trust your own instincts and go for ones that look, feel and smell really good. It's also quite wise to become chummy with your fishmonger – find out when the freshest fish comes in, then make sure he reserves it for you.

Whole Roasted Salmon Wrapped in Herbs and Newspaper

This recipe is absolutely great for parties. It's a fantastic way of cooking pretty much any whole fish, particularly salmon and trout. It's best cooked on a camp fire, over a barbecue or in a wood oven, as the paper will begin to burn, giving you a fantastic subtle smoked flavour. You will still get great results from cooking in a conventional oven but the newspaper will not blacken as on a camp fire. This recipe varies very little, depending on the number of people that you want to serve – for more than 6, just use a bigger salmon, more herbs, more paper and a slightly longer cooking time.

SERVES 6

1 x 1.5kg/3½lb whole salmon, scaled and gutted • sea salt and freshly ground black pepper • olive oil • 4 large handfuls of mixed fresh herbs (parsley, fennel tops, basil) • a copy of *The Times* (or your regular paper!) • 2 lemons, thinly sliced • 6 spring onions, thinly sliced • 2 tablespoons fennel seeds, cracked

Get yourself a nice fresh salmon, season inside and out, rub with olive oil and stuff with half the herbs. Open your paper out to the middle page and place your salmon in the centre. Scatter over your lemons, spring onions, fennel seeds and remaining herbs. Tuck some of these underneath and over the salmon. Drizzle with a little extra olive oil, tuck in the sides of the paper and fold to wrap up tightly, securing it well with lots of string. Wet the paper really well under the tap and either place directly on a shelf at the top of your oven, preheated to 220°C/425°F/gas 7, for 35 minutes, or preferably cook on your barbie or on a rack over a camp fire for about 25 minutes on each side depending on the intensity of the heat.

Salmon is a good fish for this recipe because it's quite fatty, so whether it's still a bit pink or slightly overdone it's still very acceptable. I like it slightly pink, served with some boiled potatoes, green salad and homemade mayonnaise – fantastic.

Essex Oysters Freshly Shucked on Bashed-up Ice – My Favourite Ways

Oysters are funny old things. Now they're considered a decadent aphrodisiac, when only 100 years ago they were the pigeons of the sea and would be chucked into pies as peasant food. Aphrodisiac? I'm not sure, but I do seem to have acquired a taste for them over the last 3 years.

I've eaten oysters all round the world and everyone seems to think that theirs are the best – well, I'll join the patriotic club and say that the best oysters I've ever eaten in my life are West Mersea Essex native oysters, sometimes known as Colchester oysters, along with some West Irish oysters that have a beautiful iron and subtle seawatery taste. The oysters directly from West Mersea are fantastic because they are farmed a couple of miles down the estuary where Maldon sea salt comes from. The nutrients from the marshland are leached out when the rain falls on it and are later drained into the estuary, so it's a fantastically nutritious area. I'll always go for small oysters because, quite frankly, I can't handle the big ones.

But no matter what kind of oysters you have, here's two fantastic ways to knock them back. You can get your fishmonger to open the oysters for you or you can freshly shuck (open) them with a small knife or oyster-shucker, using a tea towel to hold them (see pictures opposite), eat them the day that you buy them and serve them on some ice cubes that you've bashed up in a tea towel.

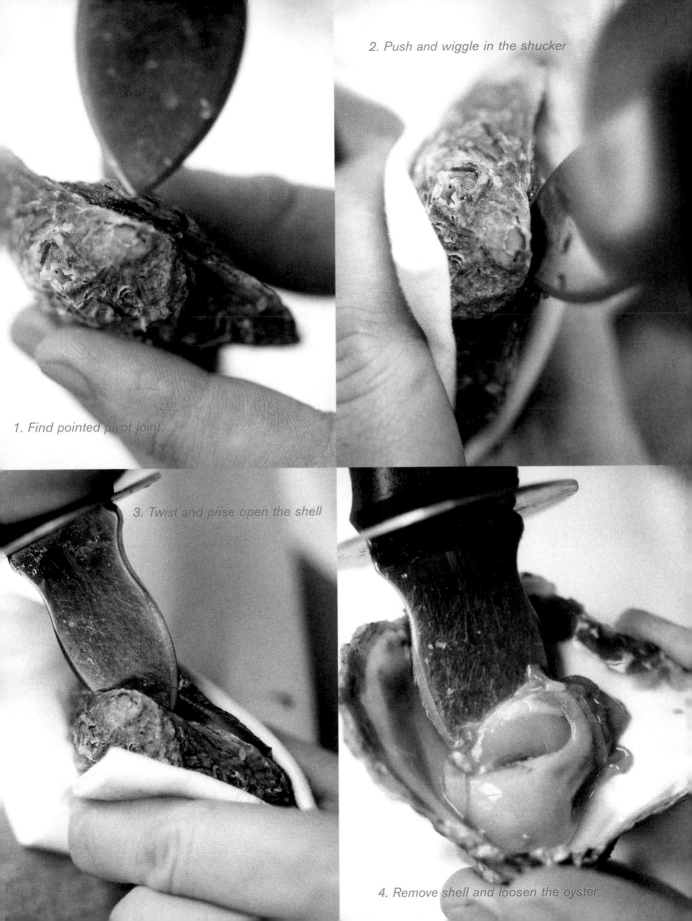

1. Find pointed pivot joint

2. Push and wiggle in the shucker

3. Twist and prise open the shell

4. Remove shell and loosen the oyster

Oysters with Shallots and Red Wine Vinegar

Finely chop 1 peeled shallot and mix with 2 heaped teaspoons of sugar, 6 tablespoons of red wine vinegar and a little pepper. Allow to sit for 10 minutes. Serve in a dish with the oysters.

Oysters with Chilli, Ginger and Rice Wine Vinegar

Finely grate ½ a thumb-sized piece of peeled ginger and mix with
6 tablespoons of rice wine vinegar, 1 finely chopped and deseeded
red chilli and a little finely sliced fresh coriander.
Stir in a teaspoon of sugar until
dissolved. Serve in a dish with
the oysters.

Seared Tuna with Grated Ginger and Chives

This is pretty much simplicity at its best. I had this in a sushi bar in Tokyo and loved being able to appreciate the deep red fresh bluefin tuna. It is just a matter of very quickly searing the fish, then mopping it through a little soy sauce, ginger and chives and whopping it straight in your choppers.

SERVES 4

225–285g/8–10oz best bluefin tuna, preferably the tail end
or a thin strip of the loin • soy sauce • 1 tablespoon sesame
oil • 2 thumb-sized pieces of fresh ginger • 1 bunch
of fresh chives, finely sliced

Marinate your tuna in a little soy sauce for 1 hour. Pat dry with kitchen paper, rub with the sesame oil and sear for around 2 minutes in a very hot non-stick frying pan, turning regularly. Allow to sit for 1 minute while you peel and finely grate the ginger. To serve, place a little blob of fresh ginger and a small pile of chives on one side of each plate, with a pool of soy sauce in the middle. Using a sharp knife, cut the tuna into ½–1cm slices, giving each person at least 3 or 4 pieces. In Japan, thicker slices are considered a sign of generosity and real decadence but I still like them quite thin.

Sicilian Roasted Brill Steak with Lemon, Anchovies, Capers and Rosemary

This is a fantastic way to eat meaty white fish like brill, turbot and halibut. It's really special if they are cut through the bone into tranches (steaks) – a nice fillet will do as well. Ask your fishmonger to cut you the steaks. You can get hold of Sicilian lemons in some supermarkets now.

SERVES 4

1 handful of fresh rosemary, leaves picked • extra virgin olive oil • 4 x 200g/7oz brill, turbot or halibut tranches/steaks • sea salt and freshly ground black pepper • 2 large unwaxed lemons, finely sliced • 1 large handful of salted capers, soaked • 8 good anchovy fillets • a splash of white wine or prosecco

Preheat the oven to 200°C/400°F/gas 6. Bruise your rosemary in a pestle and mortar to bring out the flavour. Add 6 tablespoons of extra virgin olive oil and scrunch together. Pat half of this flavoured oil round the fish, season well and put into an earthenware dish or roasting tray. Lay 4 or 5 thin slices of lemon over each steak (I normally slice these on a mandolin or use a very sharp knife). Sprinkle over your capers, and drape over your anchovies. Drizzle with the remaining flavoured oil and bake in the preheated oven for around 15 minutes off the bone or 25 minutes on the bone. Now you could splash a little wine in if you like. Remove from the oven and allow to rest, just like a steak, for 5 minutes. Sometimes I like to squeeze a little extra lemon juice over the fish so it can mix with the white creamy cooking juice and olive oil, making an amazing natural sauce. Great served with any steamed greens or a good crispy salad.

Rosemary Skewered Monkfish with Pancetta and Bread

This is a forever-winning combo that involves the slightly unusual marriage between meat and fish. It works out pretty cost-effective as well, because you're using less fish than you normally would and you're actually making it taste a lot more interesting too. Give it a bash.

SERVES 4

455g/1lb trimmed monkfish tail or any meaty white fish • 1½ ciabatta loaves, crusts removed • 4 x 25cm/10 inch fresh rosemary twigs • 1 clove of garlic, peeled • extra virgin olive oil • sea salt and freshly ground black pepper • 12 rashers of pancetta or smoked streaky bacon • 1–2 tablespoons good balsamic vinegar

Preheat the oven to 220°C/425°F/gas 7. Cut the monkfish into 2.5cm/1-inch dice and add to a bowl with the ciabatta, ripped up into similar-sized pieces. Keeping the top 5cm/2 inches of rosemary leaves, run your thumb and forefinger down the length of the stalk, removing all the leaves. Throw these into a pestle and mortar and bash up with the garlic. Then stir in 5 or 6 tablespoons of extra virgin olive oil. Pour this over your monkfish and bread and toss around.

Now begin to skewer the kebabs. At an angle, slice the tip off the rosemary stalks, so they are sharp. Put a piece of monkfish on first, then bread, and repeat until you have about 3 pieces of monkfish and about 3 pieces of bread on each kebab and lightly season. Loosely wrap 3 pieces of pancetta round each kebab, weaving it in and around the fish and the bread. Place the kebabs on a roasting tray, sprinkle with any leftover oil and rosemary, and bake in the preheated oven for 15–20 minutes, until the bread is crisp and golden. Drizzle a little balsamic vinegar over each piece of monkfish, then a little extra olive oil and any juice from the tray. Serve simply with a good salad. Happy days!

Prawns with Chilli, Parsley, Ginger and Garlic on Toast

This is a really quick dinner which always hits the spot. Nice to do as a starter as well. Just put some finger-bowls on the table and let your mates dive in. I always put a little extra chilli in and make sure I've got some nice cold wine on the go as well.

SERVES 4

extra virgin olive oil • 1 thumb-sized piece of fresh ginger, peeled and finely chopped • 2 cloves of garlic, peeled and finely sliced • 2–3 fresh red chillies, deseeded and finely sliced • 16 large whole raw tiger prawns, tails left on or peeled off • 1–2 lemons, to taste • 1 good handful of fresh flat-leaf parsley, roughly chopped • sea salt and freshly ground black pepper • 4 long slices of ciabatta bread, toasted

Into a large, hot frying pan put around 4 tablespoons of olive oil, your ginger, garlic, chilli and prawns. Fry for about 3 minutes, then turn the heat down and squeeze in the juice of 1 lemon. Add the parsley and a couple of lugs of olive oil. Toss over and remove from the heat. You should have a nice juicy sauce – have a taste. It may need a little more lemon juice. Season to taste. Serve over your ciabatta, to mop up the juices.

Lovely Tray-baked Plaice with Spinach, Olives and Tomatoes

Another great tray-baked recipe which is perfect for coping with lots of people without a huge deal of effort. You can use any similar flat fish, like lemon sole, instead of plaice.

SERVES 4

extra virgin olive oil • 2 cloves of garlic, peeled and sliced •
1 wineglass of Chardonnay • 2 x 400g/14oz tins of plum
tomatoes • 150g/5½oz black olives, stoned • 1 large handful
of fresh basil • 2 anchovy fillets • 4 x 200g/7oz plaice fillets,
skin removed • sea salt and freshly ground black pepper •
4 rosemary twigs or cocktail sticks • 3 large handfuls of
baby spinach, washed

Preheat the oven to 200°C/400°F/gas 6. Use a small roasting tray, so the fish cooks snugly. Put the tray over a medium heat on the hob, add a little olive oil, and slowly fry your sliced garlic until softened. Before it colours, add the wine and cook for 1 minute, then add your tomatoes. Break these up with a spoon, then turn down to a simmer while you prepare your plaice.

Finely chop or purée your olives, basil and anchovy fillets in a Magimix food processor, then add olive oil to loosen, giving you a spreadable paste. On a board, lay the plaice fillets down on what was their skin side and season with black pepper. Divide the paste into 4 and smear all over the fillets. Roll each fillet up like a Swiss roll from the tail end and secure with a spiked piece of rosemary, or use a cocktail stick, to hold it together. Season the tomato sauce, then place the fish fillets next to each other on top of the sauce. Drizzle with olive oil and bake in the preheated oven for 15 minutes. The sauce will flavour the plaice and vice versa, which is great.

Remove the fish to 4 warmed plates and place the sauce back on the hob for 1 minute, while you throw in your spinach – it will wilt quickly. Spoon your spinachy sauce next to the fish and get stuck in. Beautiful.

Magnificent Roasted Monkfish

The whole idea behind this recipe was to be able to make something really quick and ultra-tasty and present it in a way that looked like you'd been working for hours on it. As monkfish comes in different sizes, feel free to do individual 200g/7oz fillets or to cook a whole larger fillet and divide it up once cooked. So, here goes.

SERVES 4

1 small jar of sun-dried tomatoes in oil • 2 large handfuls
of fresh basil • olive oil • 16–20 slices of Parma ham •
4 x 200g/7oz monkfish tail fillets, trimmed • sea salt and
freshly ground black pepper • optional: balsamic
vinegar and rocket, to serve

Preheat the oven to 200°C/400°F/gas 6. Place your sun-dried tomatoes and half their flavoursome preserving oil in a Magimix food processor with all your basil and blend until smooth. While blending, I add the remaining preserving oil to the paste until it's nice and spreadable. Sometimes even a dash of balsamic vinegar is quite nice to flavour and loosen.

You are going to need 4 A4-sized pieces of greaseproof paper. Rub some olive oil over each piece of greaseproof paper and lay about 4 slices of Parma ham snugly next to each other, on each piece of paper. Divide your paste into 4, smearing each part evenly over the ham. Then place your monkfish fillets at one end, season, and, using the greaseproof paper, fold and roll up. Remove the greaseproof paper and carefully move to an oiled baking tray or dish, then roast in the pre-heated oven for 15–20 minutes.

I like to slice the fish up and serve it with some really buttery mashed potato, thinned down with lots of milk. And maybe drizzle a little balsamic vinegar over the fish, and scatter a little rocket over the whole plate.

Fried and Roasted Skate Wings with Lemon and Five-spice Salt

There's nothing better than a good piece of fresh skate but this method of cooking always cheers me up. It's still as moreish and lovely as skate always is, but the lemon and five-spice liven it up and make it quite exciting. A good little trick is to use a pair of scissors or a sharp knife and remove the flimsy edges of the wings as these will only curl up and burn anyway.

SERVES 4

zest of 1 lemon, finely chopped • 1 teaspoon five-spice • 2 heaped teaspoons Maldon sea salt • 4 x 225g/8oz very fresh skate wings • a couple of handfuls of flour, to dust • 2 eggs, lightly beaten • 6 good handfuls of fine breadcrumbs • olive oil

Preheat the oven to 220°C/425°F/gas 7. Put your lemon zest, five-spice and salt into a pestle and mortar. Bash up and mix around, then sprinkle over both sides of your skate wings. Get 3 large plates out and put your flour on one, your eggs on another and your breadcrumbs on the third. Put a large non-stick pan on a high heat and add 1cm/½ inch of olive oil. Working quickly, dip both sides of each wing first into the flour, shaking off any excess, then into the eggs, allowing the excess to drip off. Next press them firmly into the breadcrumbs, shaking off the excess.

Fry the skate wings, either 1 or 2 at a time, in the hot oil for 2 minutes on each side until lightly golden. Place on a large roasting tray while you fry the remaining fish, changing the oil if necessary. When all 4 skate wings are done, place the roasting tray in the middle of the preheated oven for 15 minutes, by which time the fish should be golden and crisp and the meat should just pull away from the bone.

I normally serve this with a light herb salad and a dollop of flavoured mayonnaise. Simply mix 4 tablespoons of mayonnaise, or crème fraîche, with 2 handfuls of chopped spring onions and chopped fresh coriander and the juice of 1 lime.

Pan-seared Scallops with Asparagus and Baby Leeks

I've come across a couple of fantastic revelations here that I want to tell you about. First, by scoring the scallops on one side in a criss-cross fashion they open out when seared like a beautiful flower and when drizzled with a little dressing or sauce they take in all the flavour. Second, the subtle use of five-spice with any seafood is a real pleasure.

SERVES 4

16 asparagus spears, trimmed • 12 baby leeks • extra virgin olive oil • sea salt and freshly ground black pepper • 1 handful of fresh marjoram or summer savory, leaves picked • 1 lemon • 12 large scallops, trimmed • 2 pinches five-spice • butter

Blanch your asparagus and leeks in salted boiling water for a couple of minutes or until just tender and drain. Get a large, non-stick frying pan hot, then drizzle with olive oil. Cook your asparagus and leeks in batches if need be – they should cover the bottom of the pan in a single layer. Season and cook until lightly coloured on all sides. Remove to a bowl and rip over half your herbs. Add a squeeze of lemon juice. Leave to one side while you cook your scallops.

Get the same pan nice and hot, score the scallops half-way through in a criss-cross fashion on one side, season them on both sides with some salt, pepper and the five-spice, drizzle the pan with a few lugs of olive oil and add your scallops. Fry for a couple of minutes until they are golden, flip them over, add the rest of your herbs and cook for 1 more minute.

While the scallops are cooking, divide your leeks and asparagus between 4 warmed plates. Remove the pan from the heat and add 2 good knobs of butter and the juice of ½ the lemon. Shake the pan about, then put 3 scallops and a little bit of juice on to each plate. Serve immediately and get stuck in.

Wicked Baked Sardines

My inspiration for this dish came from the lovely Rose Gray at the River Café, where she would do fantastic things with sardines. The great thing about these is that you can have two or three for a snack, or just one as an appetizer. Feel free to improvise around the herb and breadcrumb story. Scrumptious, mate.

PS Get your fishmonger to prepare the fillets for you.

SERVES 4

1 small bulb of fennel, with leafy tops • 1 stale ciabatta loaf, crusts removed • 1 handful of pinenuts, lightly toasted • 1 handful of fresh marjoram, leaves picked • sea salt and freshly ground black pepper • extra virgin olive oil • 8 slices of pancetta or dry-cured smoked bacon rashers • 8 fresh sardines, scaled, gutted and filleted • 8 rosemary twigs or cocktail sticks

Remove the leafy tops and stalk from the fennel. Put the leafy bits to one side and discard the stalks. Halve the fennel bulb, and finely chop. Whizz up the ciabatta to coarse breadcrumbs in a food processor or finely chop with a knife, and put the crumbs into a bowl with the fennel, pinenuts and marjoram. Season well and mix in 4 or 5 tablespoons of olive oil.

Preheat the oven to 220°C/425°F/gas 7. On a clean board, lay out 1 slice of pancetta. Place a sardine fillet, skin-side down, across it at right angles. Sprinkle the sardine with some of the breadcrumb mix, place another sardine fillet, skin-side up, on top of it, sprinkle with a little more breadcrumb mix, then tightly wrap the pancetta around it and spike with a rosemary twig or cocktail stick. Repeat until you have 8 small sardine sandwiches. Lay them on oiled greaseproof paper in a roasting tray and roast at the top of the preheated oven for 8 minutes or until the bacon and breadcrumbs are crisp.

Serve with a little rocket salad, a wedge of lemon, and sprinkle with the green fennel tops. And lads, if you can't pull the birds with that, you might as well give up now!

Roasted Red Mullet Stuffed with Breadcrumbs, Sun-dried Tomatoes, Olives, Pinenuts and Marjoram

A lovely way of livening up what is really a simple piece of roasted fish. It might be worth you cooking an extra fish so that the next day you can remove it from the bone, tear it up, toss it with some green leaves, oil and lemon and serve on some toasted bruschetta. A nice little starter.

SERVES 4

½ a ciabatta loaf • 1 large handful of sun-dried tomatoes, chopped • 1 large handful of olives, destoned and chopped • 1 large handful of pinenuts • 1 handful of fresh marjoram or basil, leaves picked • olive oil • sea salt and freshly ground black pepper • 4 x 225g/8oz whole red mullet, scaled, gutted and scored

Preheat your oven to 200°C/400°F/gas 6. Remove the crusts from your ciabatta and either whizz the bread up in a food processor until you have small but coarse breadcrumbs, or use a knife to chop the bread finely. Put the bread into a bowl with the sun-dried tomatoes, olives, pinenuts and marjoram and mix together, loosening with a couple of lugs of olive oil.

Season the fish inside and out and place on an oiled baking tray or pan. Stuff the insides with the bread mixture, pushing some into the scored slits and sprinkling any extra around the fish. Roast at the top of the oven for around 20 minutes until the fish is cooked. Serve, ideally, with a crisp green salad — I normally sprinkle the excess breadcrumbs over the salad as well (how orgasmic is that?!).

NICE BIT OF MEAT ... At the weekend it's definitely worth getting in some really nice organic meat and spoiling yourself, family and friends. When I buy meat I'm always tempted to buy a little more than I need, so I can use the scrumptious leftovers to make sandwiches, stews, soups or things like shepherd's pie. This chapter contains some of my favourite meat dishes, with inspiration from all around the world. There's nothing better than having a load of mates round for dinner and serving up the tastiest roast. Have a little flick through and see what takes your fancy – there are some really simple recipes as well as some quite indulgent ones too.

Slow-roasted Duck with Sage, Ginger and Rhubarb Homemade Sauce

This is one of the best duck recipes I've ever had. Slow-roasting means the skin goes really crispy and you cook out loads of fat (which you can keep in the fridge or freezer for roasting your potatoes in the future), and the meat becomes tender, sticky and fantastically rich.

SERVES 4

2 x 1.5kg/3½lb Gresham, Aylesbury or mallard ducks • salt and freshly ground black pepper • 255g/9oz fresh ginger • 2 long sticks of baby rhubarb • 2 handfuls of fresh sage, roughly chopped • 1 bulb of garlic, cloves removed and chopped in half • 2 red onions, finely sliced • 2 wineglasses Marsala or Vin Santo • 285ml/½ pint vegetable, chicken or duck stock • olive oil

Preheat the oven to 180°C/350°F/gas 4. Season your ducks generously inside and out. Coarsely grate half your ginger and rhubarb. Mix this in a bowl with half of your sage and all the garlic and onion, and stuff inside the cavity of your ducks. Place them on a tray and roast in the oven for 1 hour, then turn the temperature down to 150°C/300°F/gas 2 and cook for another hour and a half until crisp and tender. During this cooking time, you'll need to drain the fat maybe 3 times into a bowl – it will separate into clear fat which you can keep for roasting. The ducks are ready when the skin is crisp and the leg bones can be easily loosened.

Once cooked, allow the ducks to rest on a warmed plate while you make the sauce. Drain off any remaining fat from the roasting tray. Pull out all the stuffing and any juices from the inside of the ducks into the roasting tray. Heat the roasting tray on a low heat, add your Marsala and loosen all the sticky goodness from the bottom of the tray. This may flame so mind your eyebrows. Add your stock and reduce to a good taste and consistency. Pass through a coarse sieve. With a knife you can easily remove the breasts from the ducks and, using your hands, remove the thighs. Divide on to plates. To finish off, finely slice the remaining ginger and fry off in a little hot oil in a non-stick frying pan. As it begins to colour, add the rest of your rhubarb, finely sliced, and finish with the rest of the sage until crisp. Sprinkle this over the duck and drizzle with your tasty sauce.

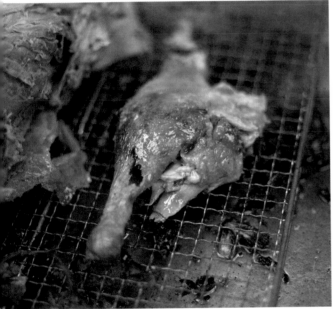

Pot-roasted Pork in White Wine with Garlic, Fennel and Rosemary

This pork recipe takes me about 5 minutes to prepare and get in the oven, so it's nice and quick as well as being unbelievably light, fresh and tasty. Also, pot-roasting the pork as opposed to straight roasting gives you a lovely natural sauce made with the meat juices and the wine.

SERVES 6

1 x 1.5kg/3½lb loin of pork, off the bone and skin
removed • salt and freshly ground black pepper • 1 tablespoon
fennel seeds • 2–3 large knobs of butter • olive oil •
8 cloves of garlic, skin left on • 1 handful of fresh rosemary,
leaves picked • 4 bay leaves • 1 fennel bulb, sliced
• ½ a bottle of Chardonnay, your choice

Preheat the oven to 200°C/400°F/gas 6. With 2 or 3 bits of string, tie up your pork loin (see pictures opposite) – do this any way you like. It doesn't have to be fussy, you just want to keep the meat in a snug shape while it's cooking. Season generously, then roll the meat in the fennel seeds until covered. In a casserole pan or roasting tray, fry the meat for a couple of minutes in half the butter and a little olive oil, until nice and golden.

Throw in the garlic, herbs, fennel and wine, then cover the tray loosely with some wet greaseproof paper and place in the oven for 1¼ hours. As the pork loin is off the bone it cooks very quickly. Remove from the oven and allow the meat to rest on a plate. Then, without using any more heat, finish off your sauce in the pan, scraping any goodness off the bottom and adding the rest of the butter. Remove any large bits of rosemary stalk if you prefer – but I like to keep it nice and rustic. Correct the seasoning and squash open a couple of the garlic cloves – when cooked they go nice and sweet and add a lovely taste to the sauce.

Superb Marinated Pork Fillet Roasted on Rhubarb

This dish always surprises people when I serve it to them. The pork fillet doesn't take long to cook, and by roasting it on the rhubarb you'll get fantastic flavours and a superb juice. An excellent accompaniment to the rich meat, just like apple sauce.

SERVES 4

1 large handful of fresh sage • 2 cloves of garlic, peeled •
olive oil • 2 pork fillets, trimmed • sea salt and freshly ground
black pepper • 10 slices of prosciutto or Parma ham •
12 long sticks of baby rhubarb, washed

First bash up half your sage in a pestle and mortar or use a metal bowl with a rolling pin. Add your garlic and smash. Add 5 tablespoons of olive oil, then rub the mixture all over your pork fillets and allow to marinate for an hour if possible (I've been known to cook the meat straight away, so it's not the end of the world if you haven't got time on your hands).

Preheat the oven to 220°C/425°F/gas 7. Lightly season the pork and drape 5 slices of prosciutto over each fillet – any excess marinade can be rubbed on to this as well. Cut your rhubarb into finger-sized pieces and place in an appropriately-sized roasting tray (preferably not aluminium, as it will taint the rhubarb). Place the pork on top of the rhubarb, almost tucking it into bed! Sprinkle over the rest of your sage leaves and drizzle with olive oil. Get yourself a piece of greaseproof paper, wet it and scrunch it up. Then lay it over the meat and tuck it in round the sides. Cook in the preheated oven for 15 minutes, then remove the paper and cook for an extra 15 minutes.

Remove from the oven and leave to rest for about 5 minutes. I slice the meat at an angle, giving each person half a fillet each. Pour any juice that comes out of the meat back into the roasting tray. Serve the meat with the rhubarb, the lovely juices from the tray and roast potatoes.

Flour and Water Crust Chicken

This is a great dish to serve up to friends – they'll wonder if you've gone a bit mad when you produce what looks like a huge lump of pastry and put it in the middle of the table! It's a great way to cook chicken – the meat steams inside the pastry crust and becomes incredibly tender. I've used nice small spring chickens, or poussins, in this recipe but it's just as easy to use one 2kg/4½lb bird and roast it for 2 hours instead. PS You don't eat the pastry!

SERVES 4

905g/2lb plain flour • 2 fat lemons • 2 handfuls of fresh sage, leaves picked • 1 handful of fresh thyme, leaves picked • 8 cloves of garlic • 8 tablespoons olive oil • sea salt and freshly ground black pepper • 4 spring chickens

Put your flour into a large bowl, and mix in around 500ml/18fl oz of water, bit by bit, until you have a dough that is pliable and elastic and not too sticky. Cover and put to one side while you prepare the chickens.

Using a peeler, remove the peel from 1 of the lemons and bash up with the sage, thyme and garlic in a pestle and mortar, or use a metal bowl and a rolling pin. Add your olive oil and plenty of seasoning. This flavourful marinade is great with just about all kinds of meat. Roll up your sleeves and rub the marinade all over the chickens as well as inside the cavity. Slice the remaining lemon and stick a slice or two inside the cavity of each chicken.

Preheat the oven to 220°C/425°F/gas 7. Get your dough mix, divide it into 4 pieces, and roll each one out to about 0.5cm/¼ inch thick. Now mould a piece of dough around each of the chickens so that you have 4 airtight parcels. Leave for 5 minutes, then bake in the preheated oven for an hour. The crust will harden during cooking, steaming and protecting the chicken while keeping all the lovely juices inside which will give you a fantastic homemade gravy.

Let the chickens rest for 15 minutes after baking, then bring them to the table and, for a bit of drama, crack open each crust in front of your guests. You'll unleash a wicked aroma, steam, the lot, so waft it around a bit. Very impressive stuff. Serve simply with some potatoes and greens.

Pot-roasted Chicken with Sweet and Sour Sauce

This is a fantastic but slightly tacky-sounding roast chicken dish. I have to keep reinventing chicken dishes, as Jools makes me cook chicken every Sunday. It starts to do my head in a bit, but this is one of my latest little winners that always puts a smile on her funny little face.

SERVES 4

1 x 2kg/4½lb chicken, preferably organic • sea salt and freshly ground black pepper • 1 handful of fresh parsley, roughly chopped • 4 thumb-sized pieces of fresh ginger, grated with skin left on • 2 red peppers, halved and deseeded • 2 yellow peppers, halved and deseeded • 4 red onions, peeled • 2 fresh chillies, snapped in half • 1 ripe pineapple, peeled, quartered and chopped • 1 teaspoon fennel seeds, crushed • olive oil • 2 tablespoons sugar • 6 tablespoons balsamic vinegar

Preheat the oven to 190°C/375°F/gas 5. Season your chicken generously inside and out and stuff the cavity with the mixed parsley and ginger. Cut your peppers and red onions into quarters and put them into a cold casserole pan. Add the chillies, pineapple and crushed fennel seeds. Drizzle with 3 good lugs of olive oil, sprinkle with salt and pepper, and toss until well-coated. Place your chicken on top, pat it with a little oil and cook in the middle of the preheated oven for 1½ hours. The chicken is ready when the bones can easily be pulled out of the thighs.

Once cooked, drain the chicken juices over the pan. Remove the chicken to a plate with half of the vegetables and pineapple, and allow to rest for 5 minutes while you make your sauce. Put the remaining vegetables and pineapple from the pan into a food processor with the sugar and balsamic vinegar, and correct the seasoning with a little salt. Blend to make a lovely sauce – add a little boiling water to loosen and thin out if need be. You could pass it through a coarse sieve to make it even smoother, but I don't. Season to taste.

To be honest, I can't think of anything better to serve the chicken with than some simple stir-fried noodles or some steamed or boiled rice. Just put the chicken and the veg in the middle of the table and tuck in.

Chicken in Salt with Fennel, Thyme and Lemon

Possibly the maddest recipe in the world and, before you think it, this is not over-salty. It's probably one of the most luxurious chicken dishes you can have. Your friends will think you've lost it when you come out to the table with a block of salt and a pickaxe (joke).

SERVES 4

3kg/7lb coarse rock salt • 8 heaped tablespoons whole fennel seeds, cracked • 2 eggs, beaten • 2 lemons, halved • 1 tablespoon peppercorns • 1 bunch of fresh thyme • olive oil • 1 x 2kg/4½lb organic chicken • 1 bunch of parsley, ripped • 8 cloves of garlic, skins left on, squashed

Preheat the oven to 200°C/400°F/gas 6. Put all the salt into a bowl with the fennel seeds, eggs, lemon juice (keep the skins), peppercorns and a wineglass of water and mix together. Bash up the thyme in a pestle and mortar and add a couple of good lugs of olive oil. Scrunch it up and rub this flavoured oil all over your chicken, finally pushing any excess inside the cavity along with your parsley, garlic and squeezed lemon halves. The idea here is to tightly pack the cavity so it bulges and no salt can get in.

Get 4 long pieces of tin-foil and put them on top of each other to make a sheet around a metre/39 inches square. Lay on a third of the salt, making it about 2cm/¾ inch thick. Put your chicken on top, then pack the rest of the salt around it. Because the salt is slightly wet it should stick to the chicken – make sure that the chicken's skin hasn't been pierced. Carefully fold up the sides of the tin-foil and scrunch it at the top. You can rip off any excess tin-foil – basically the foil is there to hold the salt together until it hardens.

Place the chicken in the preheated oven and cook for 2 hours, then remove from the oven and allow to rest for 15 minutes. Take it to the table with one or two really nice salads, some bread and a bottle of white. Rip open the tin-foil and crack the salt crust. It will fall apart easily and reveal the fantastic-smelling chicken. Pull the skin away and tear the meat from the thighs and the breast – absolutely pukka. Gorgeous served with horseradish mixed with crème fraîche or with some home-made basil mayonnaise.

Chicken in Milk

A slightly odd but really fantastic combination which must be tried.

SERVES 4

1 x 1.5kg/3½lb organic chicken • salt and freshly ground
black pepper • 115g/4oz or ½ a pack of butter • olive oil •
½ a cinnamon stick • 1 good handful of fresh sage,
leaves picked • zest of 2 lemons • 10 cloves of garlic,
skin left on • 565ml/1 pint milk

Preheat the oven to 190°C/375°F/gas 5, and find a snug-fitting pot for the chicken. Season it generously all over, and fry it in the butter and a little olive oil, turning the chicken to get an even colour all over, until golden. Remove from the heat, put the chicken on a plate, and throw away the oil and butter left in the pot. This will leave you with tasty sticky goodness at the bottom of the pan which will give you a lovely caramelly flavour later on.

Put your chicken back in the pot with the rest of the ingredients, and cook in the preheated oven for 1½ hours. Baste with the cooking juice when you remember. The lemon zest will sort of split the milk, making a sauce which is absolutely fantastic.

To serve, pull the meat off the bones and divide it on to your plates. Spoon over plenty of juice and the little curds. Serve with wilted spinach or greens and some mashed potato.

My Old Man's Superb Chicken

SERVES 4

170g/6oz mushrooms, any combination • olive oil • 1 or 2
cloves of garlic, peeled and finely chopped • salt and freshly
ground black pepper • 1 handful of fresh flat-leaf parsley,
chopped • 4 x 200g/7oz skinless chicken breasts •
1 x 500g/1lb 2oz pack of puff pastry • 1 egg, beaten •
2 heaped tablespoons wholegrain mustard • 1 large wineglass
of white wine • 140ml/5fl oz double cream

Preheat the oven to 200°C/400°F/gas 6. Chop up the mushrooms – half rough and half fine. To a hot pan, add a couple of lugs of olive oil and slowly fry the garlic with the mushrooms for about 10 minutes. Season to taste and stir in the chopped parsley. Allow to cool. Pull back the chicken fillet on the breast and, keeping it intact, score into the breast and stuff the chicken with the cooled mushrooms (see pictures opposite).

Using a little dusting of flour and a rolling pin, roll the pastry out to around 45cm/18 inches in length, 20cm/8 inches wide and just over 0.5cm/¼ inch thick. Slice into 4 pieces, lengthways, and wrap around each chicken breast (see pictures below). Brush the pastry with a little egg, and cook in the preheated oven for 35 minutes. While the chicken is cooking, put the mustard and white wine into a hot pan and allow to reduce until you've cooked away the alcohol smell. Add the cream and simmer until the sauce coats the back of a spoon, then remove from the heat and season to taste. Slice each chicken breast into 3 and serve with a bit of sauce and a little drizzle of olive oil if you like. Bloomin' gorgeous.

Pan-roasted Guinea Fowl with Pomegranates and Spinach

SERVES 2

1 x 1kg/2lb 3oz guinea fowl, chicken or pheasant, organic if possible • 100g/3¾oz ricotta cheese • 1 small handful of fresh thyme, leaves picked • sea salt and freshly ground black pepper • olive oil • 1 knob of butter • 1 clove of garlic, peeled and finely sliced • ½ a wineglass of white wine • seeds of 1 pomegranate, skin and yellow pith removed • 2 large handfuls of spinach, thoroughly washed

Remove the drumsticks, thighs and breasts from the bird (see pictures below) or ask your butcher to do this for you. In a small bowl, beat together your ricotta and finely chopped thyme. Season lightly. Using two fingers, delicately part the skin from the breast and the skin from the drumsticks and thighs. With a teaspoon, insert your ricotta mix into these gaps, then pull the skin down to cover up the gaps.

Preheat the oven to 220°C/425°F/gas 7. Season your guinea fowl, then drizzle an ovenproof pan with a little olive oil, and fry the drumsticks and thighs for 5 minutes until crisp and golden. Add the breasts, skin-side up, with a large knob of butter, your garlic and your wine. Place at the top of the preheated oven and cook for 25 minutes, then add the pomegranate seeds and cook for an extra 5 minutes, by which time your thigh meat will be cooked all the way through and the skin will be crispy. Take the pan out of the oven and place back on the hob. Add your spinach and let it wilt. You will have a great homemade sauce at the bottom of the pan. Check for seasoning – it should be fine – then serve a breast, thigh and drumstick on each plate with the spinach and pomegranates in and around it. Drizzle over your homemade sauce and serve with some plain boiled potatoes.

Japanese Rolled Pork with Plums, Coriander, Soy Sauce and Spring Onions

This is a fantastic appetizer that I had in Japan. With there being no fat on the pork and it being steamed, it's a very clean and tasty dish.

SERVES 4

10 plums • 2 tablespoons olive oil • 2 star anise • 2 thumb-sized pieces of fresh ginger, peeled and finely grated • 2 cloves • 2 heaped tablespoons muscovado sugar • 600g/1lb 6oz pork loin • salt and freshly ground black pepper • 1 small handful of fresh coriander, washed and chopped • spring onions • soy sauce

Wash the plums, then run a knife around them, twist them and remove the stones. Cut the halves into 1cm/½ inch dice. Heat the oil in a pan and fry the star anise, ginger and cloves for 1 minute. Add the plums and sugar with a couple of table-spoons of water, place a lid on, and simmer slowly for about 20 minutes until chunky and pulpy. Allow to cool down in the fridge.

Take your pork and trim off all the fat and sinews so that you are left with com-pletely lean eye meat. Cut into 0.5cm/¼ inch slices and one by one bash the slices between 2 pieces of clingfilm, using something flat and heavy like the base of a heavy pan, a meat hammer or a cleaver. Try to retain the pork's shape. When each piece is around the thickness of two beer mats, carefully peel the meat away from the clingfilm in one piece. Do this with all the meat and lay it out on a tray. Season the plum sauce, then stir in half the coriander. Smear a tablespoon of your sauce in the middle of each slice of pork. Spread out slightly so that the sauce covers about three-quarters of each slice and roll each one up like a Swiss roll. Put the rolls into a bamboo steamer (if you have one) or a normal steamer, or even use a colander covered in tin-foil. Place the steamer over simmering water and steam for 10–15 minutes until the meat is just cooked. Remove from the steamer and serve the pork rolls on a bed of finely sliced spring onions, sprinkled with the rest of the coriander and doused with lots of soy sauce.

The Missus xxx

Superb Roast Beef, Best Spuds and Huge Yorkies

SERVES 8

1 x 2.5kg/5½lb fore-rib, wing-rib or sirloin of beef, French-trimmed • sea salt and freshly ground black pepper • olive oil • 3 red onions, halved • 3kg/7lb roasting potatoes, peeled • 4 large parsnips, peeled and quartered • 3 rosemary twigs • 4 cloves of garlic, peeled • 2 thumb-sized pieces of fresh ginger, peeled and diced • flour • ½ a bottle of robust red wine

Roasting is easy, but timing is important. Before you start, get all your veg prepped and have your Yorkshire pudding batter made (see page 25). With this done, you can get your Yorkshires and greens on while the beef is resting out of the oven.

Preheat the oven to 230°C/450°F/gas 8, and heat a large thick-bottomed roasting tray on the hob. Rub your beef generously with salt, then add a little olive oil to the tray and lightly colour the meat for a couple of minutes on all sides. Lay your onions in the tray with the beef on top of them, then cook in the preheated oven for a total of 1½ hours. While the beef is starting parboil your potatoes in salted boiling water for around 10 minutes and drain in a colander. Toss about to chuff them up – this will make them really crispy.

After 30 minutes, take the tray out and toss in your potatoes, parsnips and rosemary. With a garlic press or grater, squeeze or grate the garlic and ginger over everything in the tray, which will taste fantastic. Shake the tray and whack it back in the oven for the final hour. Remove the potatoes and parsnips to a dish to keep warm, place the beef on a plate, covered with foil, to rest, and get your greens and Yorkshire puddings on. Preheat a Yorkshire pudding tray with 1cm/½ inch of oil in each section. After 10 minutes, divide the batter into the tray. Cook for around 30 minutes until crisp – don't open the oven door before then or they won't rise.

Remove most of the fat from your roasting tray and you should be left with caramelized onions and sticky beef goodness. Add a teaspoon of flour to the tray and mash everything together. Heat the tray on the hob and when hot, add your red wine. Simmer for 5–10 minutes, stirring every couple of minutes, until your gravy is really tasty and coats the back of a spoon. Add any juice from the beef and feel free to add some water or stock to thin the gravy if you like. Pour through a coarse sieve, pushing it through with a spoon, and serve in a warmed gravy jug.

PS Serve up your Yorkies and veg with some horseradish sauce and carve the beef at the table. Just so you know, beef needs 30 minutes per kilo to cook, plus an extra 20 minutes at the end, no matter how big it is. This will cook it medium, so give it a bit more or less depending on your preference.

Medallions of Beef with Morels and Marsala and Crème Fraîche Sauce

I always think of this as being quite a luxurious dinner. But even though it uses dried morels and medallions of beef, which are never cheap, it's a real quickie to make. Medallions of beef are basically 1cm/½ inch thick slices of beef fillet that are normally grilled or fried. You can get your butcher to prep these for you, or cut a fillet steak in half and flatten it out slightly yourself.

SERVES 4

1 handful of fresh thyme, leaves picked • 8 x 85g/3oz beef fillet medallions • olive oil • 2 handfuls of dried morels • sea salt and freshly ground black pepper • 2 shallots, peeled and finely chopped • 1 clove of garlic, peeled and finely chopped • 1 wineglass of Marsala • 4 tablespoons crème fraîche

Put your dried morels into a small bowl and cover with boiling water. Finely chop half the thyme and sprinkle over your medallion fillets with a little olive oil. Rub the thyme and oil into the meat and allow to sit for 10 minutes.

Get a large, non-stick frying pan hot, season your steaks on both sides with salt and black pepper, and sear them for just over 2 minutes on each side. They will go slightly golden and will be cooked medium by this time, which is the way I like them. Feel free to cook for longer, or less time, to your liking. Remove the meat from the pan to a plate and allow to rest for 4 or 5 minutes while you make the sauce.

Turn down the heat, add a little extra olive oil to the pan, and throw in your shallots, garlic and remaining thyme. After a minute, strain your morels and add them — I like to leave three-quarters of them whole and finely chop the rest. Add your Marsala. This may flame up in the pan for about 20 seconds, which is fine, so don't be shocked. It will smell fantastic. Add the crème fraîche and any juices that have come out of the meat. Season to taste. The sauce should coat the back of a spoon — thin it with water if it gets too thick. Give each person 2 medallions, pour the sauce over, and serve with something nice and stodgy like mashed potato, or the smashed celeriac on page 216. Also great with the braised greens on page 211.

PS If you have any thyme growing on your windowsill, snip off some of the tender new leaves and sprinkle these over the meat just before serving. An absolutely delicious thyme-fest!

Tray-baked Lamb with Aubergines, Tomatoes, Olives, Garlic and Mint Oil

SERVES 4

2 x 7-rib racks of lamb, preferably organic, French-trimmed •
2 firm aubergines • 8 ripe plum tomatoes • extra virgin
olive oil • 8 cloves of garlic, skin left on • dried oregano • sea
salt and freshly ground black pepper • optional: fresh
basil or marjoram • 1 handful olives, destoned •
1 large handful of fresh mint • a pinch
of sugar • good red wine vinegar

Preheat the oven to 200°C/400°F/gas 6. Criss-cross the fat on the lamb – this will help it render and become nice and crisp. Place to one side.

Slice your aubergines crossways into 2.5cm/1 inch thick pieces and cut your tomatoes in half. Lightly brush your aubergine slices all over with extra virgin olive oil, then fry on both sides in a non-stick pan to give them just a little colour. Remove the aubergines from the pan and place on one side of a clean roasting tray. Put your halved tomatoes and whole garlic cloves beside them and sprinkle with a little oregano and seasoning. You could always rip a little fresh basil or marjoram over the tomatoes as well.

Season the lamb and fry in your non-stick pan until lightly golden on all sides. Drizzle with a little olive oil, then place the lamb skin-side up next to your aubergines and tomatoes and bake in the preheated oven for 30 minutes to retain a little pinkness – but you can always cook it to suit your taste. Add the olives to the roasting tray for the last 5 minutes so they warm through. Remove from the oven and allow the lamb to rest for 5 minutes.

Now make some fantastic mint oil. Put the mint into either a pestle and mortar or a blender with a pinch each of salt and sugar, and blitz up until smooth. Add a couple of tablespoons of good red wine vinegar and loosen with 6 tablespoons of extra virgin olive oil. Season to taste and tweak with a little vinegar if need be. This is a fantastic sauce that is great drizzled over your veg and lamb. I like to cut my lamb in half between the ribs and then divide each half into 3 or 4 cutlets. There's always an extra rib, but that doesn't necessarily mean that someone else gets more meat than you.

PS When you buy your racks of lamb, ask your butcher to 'French-trim' them, which means that all the bones are scraped clean – this looks nice and pretty and it cooks easier as well.

... AND LOADS OF VEG People are always wondering how to completely turn around their day-to-day cooking to make things more exciting. Or maybe even a bit healthier. Here's your answer – a stonking little vegetable section. Even though I'm becoming slightly more eclectic in my old age, the Mediterranean use of vegetables and flavourings is still my favourite. My recipes in this vegetable chapter are really superb. They're quite modern British in style, with things like Minty Mushy Peas, Smashed Celeriac and World's Best Baked Onions.

When at all possible, try using some slightly more unusual vegetables because if we don't try them the shops won't keep stocking them. Over the last couple of years there's been a revolution of weekend farmers' markets. Please try to support these people as their true passion for growing and supplying excellent produce can teach us all something.

Minty Mushy Peas

This is a fantastic recipe which is so quick and so simple and uses our reliable friends the frozen peas, which work really well here. Great with fish, meat or even as a vegetarian dish with a big dollop of butter on top.

SERVES 4–6

2 medium-sized potatoes, peeled and finely diced •
1kg/2lb 3oz frozen peas • 1 handful of fresh
mint, leaves picked • 3 large knobs of butter • sea salt
and freshly ground black pepper

Boil the potatoes in salted boiling water until nearly tender. Add your peas to the pan and then after 2 minutes of boiling add the mint. After another minute, drain everything into a colander. Leave for 1 minute to steam, then put everything back into the pan and mash with a potato masher. You can do this in a Magimix food processor as well – just pulse it until smooth. Whether mashing or pulsing, when it's done add your butter and season very carefully to taste.

World's Best Baked Onions

I've found it. The best onion recipe – it's smashing, pukka, the absolute dog's kahunas! I love it served with cod but it's also great with roast chicken. You've got to try it.

SERVES 4

4 tennis-ball-sized white onions, peeled • olive oil • 2 cloves of garlic, peeled and finely chopped • 4 twigs of fresh rosemary, lower leaves picked and chopped • 8 tablespoons double cream • a couple of handfuls of grated Parmesan cheese • sea salt and freshly ground black pepper • 4 slices of pancetta or smoked streaky bacon rashers

Boil the onions in plenty of water for 15 minutes until slightly tender. Remove from the pan and allow to cool. Then, with a sharp knife, remove the top 2.5cm/1 inch of each onion, finely chop and place to one side. If need be, slightly trim the stalk end of the onions so that they will sit flat on a roasting tray. Cut about a heaped tablespoon out from the inside of each onion, keeping the outside intact. Finely chop and add to the rest of the chopped onion.

Preheat the oven to 200°C/400°F/gas 6. Heat a frying pan and add a little olive oil, your garlic, the chopped onions and just a little chopped rosemary. Fry for a couple of minutes until softened, then turn the heat down, add the cream and remove from the heat. Stir in the Parmesan and season.

I like to wrap a nice slice of pancetta around the middle of each onion and just spike it in place with a sharpened twig of rosemary or half a cocktail stick. The rosemary and pancetta will make the onion taste lovely as it cooks. Place the onions on a roasting tray and spoon some of the chopped onion mixture inside each one. Bake in the preheated oven for around 25 minutes until soft and tender, depending on the size of the onions. It's cool to experiment with different cheeses, so give it a bash.

Baked Peppers with Cherry Vine Tomatoes, Basil and Marjoram

SERVES 4

2 peppers, red or yellow • sea salt and freshly ground black pepper • 20 cherry tomatoes • 1 handful of fresh marjoram and basil • 2 cloves of garlic, peeled and sliced • extra virgin olive oil • optional: anchovies • optional: herb vinegar

Preheat the oven to 200°C/400°F/gas 6. Cut the peppers in half and remove the seeds. Place in an oiled baking dish and lightly season with salt and pepper. Prick the cherry tomatoes with a knife and place in boiling water for around 30–60 seconds until the skins can be easily and quickly pinched off. Feel free to run cold water over them before peeling. Once peeled, place the tomatoes in the peppers. Stuff in your herbs and sliced garlic and season. You could drape over some anchovies instead of using seasoning at this point. Drizzle with olive oil. Cook in the preheated oven for 15 minutes lightly covered with tin-foil, then around 30 minutes without. The smallest little splash of herb vinegar on each pepper can be a real joy – try it and see.

Braised Greens

This is a really simple and tasty way to make greens less boring. Also, having a mixture of greens makes things much more appealing. I've used three types of greens, including rocket, which is always thought of as a salad leaf. Chicoria is a slightly bitter-tasting green leaf which is excellent for braising. If you can't get hold of it then try substituting with any other type of green, like spinach, cabbage, cavolo nero, Chinese leaf, beet leaves, sprouting broccoli – whatever you fancy.

SERVES 4

2 large handfuls of Swiss chard • 2 large handfuls of chicoria or any of the leaves mentioned above • olive oil • 2 large cloves of garlic, peeled and finely sliced • sea salt and freshly ground black pepper • 2 large handfuls of rocket • ½ a lemon

Half fill a large pot with salted water, bring to the boil and add your Swiss chard and chicoria. Cook for 2 or 3 minutes until the greens are tender, or al dente, then drain in a colander. To your empty pan add 4 large glugs of olive oil and the garlic. Fry the garlic until lightly coloured, then throw in your cooked chicoria and chard. Season and stir around to coat in all the lovely flavoured oil. After 1 minute, remove from the heat, add the rocket and squeeze in the lemon juice. Stir once more, check the seasoning again, and serve immediately. Great with grilled meats or scallops, or even served cold on an antipasti plate.

Baked New Potatoes with Sea Salt and Rosemary

SERVES 4–6

1kg/2lb 3oz Jersey Royals • 1 tablespoon olive oil •
Maldon sea salt and freshly ground black pepper • 2 sprigs
of rosemary, leaves picked and bashed

Wash your potatoes and parboil until almost tender. When done, drain them, drizzle with just a little touch of olive oil and roll in a tablespoon of Maldon sea salt, a little freshly ground black pepper and the rosemary. Preheat the oven to 220°C/425°F/gas 7. Put the potatoes in a roasting tray and cook in the oven for 25 minutes until golden. Or wrap them in tin-foil and throw them on the barbie for the same amount of time.

Dad in the garden

Roasted Asparagus with Rosemary and Anchovies Wrapped in Pancetta

This is a great vegetable dish, either to have for a starter or as a vegetable with chicken or fish. Having the asparagus tied together looks damn funky and all the ingredients flavour each other as they roast in the oven, which makes them taste sensational. I've used string to tie the bundles together in the picture but it's much better to use a slice of pancetta.

SERVES 4

24 medium-sized spears of asparagus • 4 sprigs of fresh rosemary • 4 anchovy fillets • 4 good slices of pancetta or dry-cured smoky bacon rashers • ½ a lemon • olive oil • 1 knob of butter • sea salt and freshly ground black pepper

Preheat the oven to 220°C/425°F/gas 7. Remove the stalk ends of the asparagus by bending them and snapping where it clicks naturally. Feel free to boil your asparagus for a minute if they're not as tender as they should be. Grab 6 spears of asparagus, sandwich one of the rosemary sprigs and one of the anchovy fillets among the spears, and wrap a slice of pancetta round the middle to hold everything in place. Make 3 more bundles the same way, and put them into a small roasting tray or pan with ½ a lemon. Drizzle with a little olive oil and roast in the preheated oven for 4–5 minutes, until the pancetta is crispy. Remove from the oven, add your knob of butter, and squeeze over the juice of your roasted lemon. Season if need be. This will make a fantastic smoky sauce with your melted anchovies – absolutely scrumptious.

Smashed Celeriac

What a surprisingly simple and comforting veg dish. Unfortunately everyone seems to be completely baffled by celeriac, but it's beautiful in soups or thinly sliced into salads. When roasted it goes sweet and when mixed with potato and mashed it's a complete joy.

SERVES 4

1 celeriac, peeled • olive oil • 1 handful of fresh thyme, leaves picked • 2 cloves of garlic, finely chopped • sea salt and freshly ground black pepper • 3–4 tablespoons water or stock

Slice about 1cm/½ inch off the bottom of your celeriac and roll it on to that flat edge, so it's nice and safe to slice. Slice and dice it all up into 1cm/½ inch-ish cubes. Don't get your ruler out – they don't have to be perfect. Put a casserole-type pot on a high heat, add 3 good lugs of olive oil, then add the celeriac, thyme and garlic, with a little seasoning. Stir around to coat and fry quite fast, giving a little colour, for 5 minutes. Turn the heat down to a simmer, add the water or stock, place a lid on top and cook for around 25 minutes, until tender. Season carefully to taste and stir around with a spoon to smash up the celeriac. Some people like to keep it in cubes, some like to mash it, but I think it looks and tastes much better if you smash it, which is somewhere in the middle. You can serve this with just about any meat you can think of.

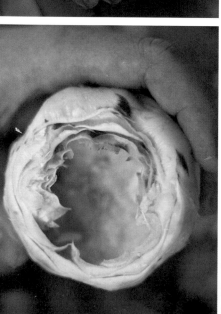
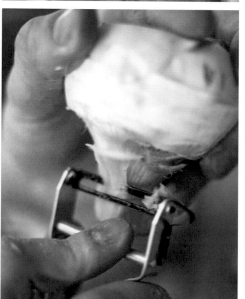

Tray-baked Artichokes with Almonds, Breadcrumbs and Herbs

This sort of veg dish is good for anything – from using as antipasti to serving with meat or fish.

SERVES 4

8 medium-sized globe artichokes • 1 lemon • 2 cloves of garlic, finely chopped • 1 handful of whole almonds, finely chopped • 2 handfuls of coarse breadcrumbs • 1 handful of fresh mint, finely chopped • 1 handful of fresh parsley, finely chopped • sea salt and freshly ground black pepper • extra virgin olive oil • 2 wineglasses of white wine

To prepare the artichokes (see pictures opposite), simply trim 5cm/2 inches below and above the base of the choke. Now what you need to do is trim back your artichoke leaves one by one, clicking them off until you get to the lovely paler yellow and more tender leaves. Using a pointed teaspoon, insert it right into the centre of the artichoke flower and slowly turn it to remove the fluffy choke. Have a little peer in and try to remove most of the choke. Rub the artichoke with lemon to stop it discolouring. You'll get the hang of it when you do the rest. You'll be left with 8 whole trimmed artichokes.

Preheat the oven to 200°C/400°F/gas 6. Toss the garlic, almonds, breadcrumbs and herbs into a bowl, season, and loosen with a little olive oil. Scrunch together with your hands and stuff this mixture into the middle of each artichoke, really packing it in. You want to fit these snugly side by side in an appropriately-sized baking dish. Sprinkle any excess filling over the top, drizzle generously with extra virgin olive oil and pour in your wine. Rip off a big enough piece of greaseproof paper, wet and scrunch it under a tap, then tuck it over the artichokes and round the edges of the dish. Bake in the preheated oven for 30 minutes, then remove the greaseproof paper and bake for a final 10 minutes. Serve in the middle of the table with seafood or any white meat.

Roasted Veg

I love roasted vegetables, and to bump up the veggies on a family dinner there's nothing better than to have 4–5 roasted ones all done in the same tray – it's completely effortless and always a treat. There are certain fresh herbs and spices that really go with certain vegetables. Feel free to flavour your veg as you like but here are my suggestions to give you a bit of a pukka edge to your veg.

All the veg should be cut into similar-sized pieces so that they cook at the same time, tossed separately with their suggested flavourings and seasoned generously. Preheat the oven to 220°C/425°F/gas 7. Place the veg in a large tray next to each other and cover with tin-foil. Cook in the preheated oven for 20 minutes, then remove the foil and continue roasting for another 20–30 minutes until the veg are golden and tender. If by any chance one is cooked before another, simply remove it from the oven and keep it warm in a serving dish.

PS You can cook as many as you like in the same tray, or just one or two. It's up to you.

- halved carrots with a pinch of cumin, rosemary and olive oil
- quartered parsnips with bashed thyme, honey and olive oil
- peeled and sliced celeriac with thyme, rosemary and olive oil
- chunks of squash with crushed coriander seeds, a hint of chilli, oregano and olive oil
- quartered fennel with its own leafy tops and olive oil
- whole baby turnips with tarragon, a splash of white wine vinegar and olive oil
- peeled and quartered red onions with sage and olive oil
- scrubbed and halved Jerusalem artichokes with marjoram, rosemary and olive oil

Roasted Fennel with Cherry Tomatoes, Olives, Garlic and Olive Oil

A great little combo that is tasty, fresh and pretty damn healthy. Any leftovers can be chopped and turned into a sexy little pasta dish, maybe with some ricotta and Parmesan cheese added to it. You could even try putting a couple of chicken breasts on top of the fennel and tomatoes before baking in the oven, to make a tasty dinner.

SERVES 6

2 bulbs of fennel • 24 cherry tomatoes • 1 large handful of pitted black olives • 1 small handful of fresh thyme, leaves picked • 2 cloves of garlic, peeled and finely sliced • sea salt and freshly ground black pepper • extra virgin olive oil • 1 wineglass of white wine, vermouth or Pernod • 2 knobs of butter

Remove the top feathery stalks from your fennel and slice them finely. Put them into a roasting tray. Cut your fennel bulbs in quarters, then cut the quarters in half. Put them into boiling, salted water and cook for 10 minutes. While your fennel is cooking, preheat the oven to 220°C/425°F/gas 7 and prick all your cherry tomatoes. After 10 minutes remove the fennel with a slotted spoon and add to the roasting tray. Add your tomatoes to the fennel water for 45 seconds, to loosen the skins. Drain them and run a little cold water over them. Pinch or peel the skins away from the tomatoes, then add the tomatoes to the roasting tray. Add the olives, thyme and garlic and season with salt and pepper. Drizzle with 2 lugs of olive oil and mix together. Try to arrange everything neatly so you have one layer. Add your wine and knobs of butter, breaking them up over the veg. Bake in the middle of the preheated oven for 30 minutes.

Swiss Chard with Cannellini Beans

SERVES 4

2 large handfuls of Swiss chard, washed • 1 small handful of
thyme or summer savory, leaves picked • 2 cloves of
garlic, peeled and thinly sliced • 2 anchovy fillets • extra virgin
olive oil • 1 x 400g/14oz tin of cannellini beans,
drained • 1 large knob of butter • sea salt and freshly
ground black pepper • ½ a lemon

Cook the Swiss chard in salted, boiling water until just tender, drain and remove to
one side. In the same pot fry your herbs, garlic and anchovies in a couple of lugs
of olive oil. Add your cannellini beans, with a tablespoon of water to help heat them
through, then after a minute add the chard and butter. Toss together and season to
taste with salt, pepper and a little squeeze of lemon juice. Serve immediately – it's
pretty good with anything.

Hamilton Squash

This is a recipe inspired by a one-minute conversation with my mate Johnny Boy Hamilton. He had basically eaten far too much meat in Paris, went for the veggie option one night and was blown away by it. His description used a marrow instead of a squash and some kind of green rice, but anyway, the great thing is I've given this a bash my way and think it's an absolutely fantastic recipe. So, nice one John. There is no need to precook the rice as it will take on moisture from being cooked inside the squash.

SERVES 4

1 small handful of dried porcini mushrooms • 1 butternut squash, halved and seeds removed • olive oil • 1 red onion, finely chopped • 1 clove of garlic, finely chopped • 1 teaspoon coriander seeds, pounded • a pinch or two of dried chilli, to taste • 2 sprigs of fresh rosemary, leaves picked and finely chopped • 5 sun-dried tomatoes, chopped • sea salt and freshly ground black pepper • 100g/3½oz basmati rice • ½ a handful of pinenuts, lightly roasted

First of all, soak your porcini for 5 minutes in 140ml/¼ pint of boiling water. Preheat the oven to 230°C/450°F/gas 8. Using a teaspoon, score and scoop out some extra flesh from the length of the squash (see pictures opposite). Finely chop this flesh with the squash seeds and add to a frying pan with 4 lugs of olive oil, the onion, garlic, coriander seeds, chilli, rosemary and sun-dried tomatoes. Fry for 4 minutes until softened. Add the porcini and half their soaking water. Cook for a further 2 minutes before seasoning. Stir in your rice and pinenuts, pack the mixture tightly into the 2 halves of the squash and then press them together. Rub the skin of the squash with a little olive oil, wrap in tin-foil, and bake in the preheated oven for about 1¼ hours.

Runner Beans with Tomato Sauce

SERVES 6

680g/1½lb runner beans, sliced diagonally into 5cm/2 inch
pieces • 2 cloves of garlic, finely chopped • a few good lugs of
extra virgin olive oil • 1 x 400g/14oz tin of chopped tomatoes
• salt and freshly ground black pepper

Steam the beans in a foil-covered colander over a pot of boiling water, or blanch in salted boiling water until tender. While they are cooking, make a quick tomato sauce: fry the garlic in some olive oil, add the tomatoes and bring to the boil, then season and simmer for about 15 minutes until you have a thick sauce. Season to taste. When the beans are cooked, stir them into the sauce.

THE WONDERFUL WORLD OF BREAD I'm still really mad about bread – I love it. It's so exciting. While me and my mate Bernie, who's a great baker, were trying to perfect our sourdough recipe it was hilarious 'cos we were like a couple of pregnant women on the phone each day seeing how our buns were proving. But that's what bread does to you. It's such a rewarding, therapeutic, tactile thing and you'll be so proud of yourself once you've cracked it.

And even though you can get all deep and cheffy about flours, fermentations and all that, I love the fact that starting from one great simple bread recipe there's a million things you can do.

Anyone can make bread. I got kids to make the bread for the step-by-step photos, because if they can do it, then surely you can too. It's easy peasy. And just to prove to you that a little fantasy can stretch a bit of plain bread a long way, here's nine fantastic breads that will get you going on a Sunday morning. Get stuck in.

Basic Bread Recipe

1kg/just over 2lb strong bread flour • 625ml/just over
1 pint tepid water • 30g/1oz fresh yeast or 3 x 7g/¼oz sachets
dried yeast • 2 tablespoons sugar • 2 level tablespoons
30g/1oz salt • extra flour for dusting

Stage 1: Making a Well

Pile the flour on to a clean surface and make a large well in the centre. Pour half
your water into the well, then add your yeast, sugar and salt and stir with a fork.

Stage 2: Getting It Together

Slowly, but confidently, bring in the flour from the inside of the well. (You don't want
to break the walls of the well, or the water will go everywhere.) Continue to bring
the flour in to the centre until you get a stodgy, porridgey consistency – then add
the remaining water. Continue to mix until it's stodgy again, then you can be more
aggressive, bringing in all the flour, making the mix less sticky. Flour your hands and
pat and push the dough together with all the remaining flour. (Certain flours need
a little more or less water, so feel free to adjust.)

Stage 3: Kneading!

This is where you get stuck in. With a bit of elbow grease, simply push, fold, slap
and roll the dough around, over and over, for 4 or 5 minutes until you have a silky
and elastic dough.

Stage 4: First Prove

Flour the top of your dough. Put it in a bowl, cover with clingfilm, and allow it to prove for about half an hour until doubled in size – ideally in a warm, moist, draught-free place. This will improve the flavour and texture of your dough and it's always exciting to know that the old yeast has kicked into action.

Stage 5: Second Prove, Flavouring and Shaping

Once the dough has doubled in size, knock the air out for 30 seconds by bashing it and squashing it. You can now shape it or flavour it as required – folded, filled, tray-baked, whatever – and leave it to prove for a second time for 30 minutes to an hour until it has doubled in size once more. This is the most important part, as the second prove will give it the air that finally ends up being cooked into your bread, giving you the really light, soft texture that we all love in fresh bread. So remember – don't fiddle with it, just let it do its thing.

Stage 6: Cooking Your Bread

Very gently place your bread dough on to a flour-dusted baking tray and into a pre-heated oven. Don't slam the door or you'll lose the air that you need. Bake according to the time and temperature given with your chosen recipe. You can tell if it's cooked by tapping its bottom – if it sounds hollow it's done, if it doesn't then pop it back in for a little longer. Once cooked, place on a rack and allow it to cool for at least 30 minutes – fandabidozi. Feel free to freeze any leftover bread.

Layered Focaccia with Cheese and Rocket

1 x basic bread recipe (see page 236) • extra virgin olive oil •
170g/6oz Parmesan cheese, grated • 200g/7oz Fontina,
Cheddar or good melting cheese, grated • 140g/5oz mild
Gorgonzola cheese, crumbled • 2 large handfuls of rocket •
1 handful of fresh marjoram, leaves picked • salt and
freshly ground black pepper • olive oil • optional: fresh
sage or thyme leaves

Follow the basic bread recipe up to Stage 5 when you are shaping the dough. Roll it into a large rectangle around 1cm/½ inch thick. Drape half of it into a medium to large flour-dusted baking tray, with half hanging over the side. On the half that is in the tray, drizzle over about 3 good lugs of extra virgin olive oil, rub it into the dough, and then add all your cheeses, your rocket, marjoram and a little seasoning. Using your fingers, push it all into the dough. Fold the overhanging dough back on to the dough in the tray and then push around the edges so that you seal them together. What I do is tuck it under so it fits nicely into the tray. Rub the top with a little olive oil and maybe rip over some fresh herbs like sage or thyme.

Leave to prove and when doubled in size, bake in your preheated oven at 180°C/350°F/gas 4 for around 25 minutes until lightly golden and cooked. Allow to sit for around 25 minutes before eating. This is a fantastic bread that can be cut into chunks, wrapped in greaseproof paper or tin-foil and kept in the freezer to be reheated when you have midnight munchies.

Gennaro Grande Cappella Rossa Calzone

My London 'father', Gennaro Contaldo, makes these to use up all his leftover antipasti. They're great — a complete snack.

MAKES 8

1 x basic bread recipe (see page 236) • 1 onion, peeled and roughly chopped • 3 cloves of garlic, peeled and finely sliced • 1 aubergine, roughly chopped • olive oil • 3 courgettes, roughly chopped • 2 x 400g/14oz tins of tomatoes • sea salt and freshly ground black pepper • optional: olives • 2 handfuls of fresh basil • 1 ball of buffalo mozzarella cheese

In a large pot, fry your onion, garlic and aubergine in a little olive oil on a high heat. After about 4 minutes, add your courgettes. Continue to fry for another 5 minutes, then add the tomatoes. Bring to the boil and simmer slowly for about 1 hour until quite thick and stodgy in texture — making sure it doesn't stick to the bottom. Remove from the heat, season well to taste, and maybe even add some olives. Once cool, rip in your basil and mozzarella.

While it's cooking, make your dough and continue through the basic bread recipe until Stage 5 where you divide the dough into 8 pieces. Roll into balls, using flour for dusting. Then roll into little frisbee shapes just over 0.5cm/¼ inch thick. Place a good spoonful of your filling into the middle of each, brush the edges with a little water, then fold the rounds in half, pushing their edges to seal. Some people prefer to use a fork to do this but I just pinch them with my fingers. Dust with flour, do the same with all the others and move to a flour-dusted baking tray. Allow to sit for 5 minutes, then score the top of the bread to allow your filling to bubble over when cooking. Bake in your preheated oven at 180°C/350°F/gas 4 for 20 minutes until golden and scrumptious-looking, and allow to cool. Always good for picnics or as portable food.

SINCE 1916

Banana and Honey Bread

1 x basic bread recipe (see page 236) • 6 bananas •
8 tablespoons good, runny honey • optional: 1 handful
of almonds, cracked or chopped

First of all, peel your bananas then purée them in a liquidizer or food processor. The mix will be surprisingly wet. Pour it into a measuring jug, then top up with water until you have 625ml or just over 1 pint. At Stage 1 of the basic bread recipe, use this banana liquid instead of the water to flavour your bread and make it nice and chewy. Also add half the honey with the nuts to the dough at this point. Then continue through the basic recipe as normal.

At Stage 5 divide the dough into 10 balls. Then pack these next to each other in a flour-dusted baking tin where they will prove together. Before putting in the oven drizzle generously with the rest of the honey so that the top of the bread will caramelize, going nice and golden. Bake in your preheated oven at 190°C/375°F/gas 5 for 20 minutes. Allow to cool for a little while, but it's best served still warm with lots of butter and a glass of milk for breakfast while you read the paper. Also fantastic used in bread and butter pudding or simply heated up with a bit of ice cream.

Walnut Bread

For this particular bread you need to use 500g wholemeal flour and 500g white flour instead of all white flour as used in the basic bread recipe. Thought I'd better make that clear.

PS When using brown or wholemeal flours you often need to add a little more water to give you an elastic, pliable dough.

1 x basic bread recipe (see page 236), using 500g/just over 1lb organic wholemeal flour and 500g/just over 1lb strong white flour • 455g/1lb good-quality walnuts, peeled • 115g/4oz dried apricots, very finely chopped • 115g/4oz butter, room temperature

At Stage 1 of the basic bread recipe remember to use both types of flour in place of just the white flour and continue to Stage 2.

Crush half of your walnuts until coarse and the other half to a fine powder. At Stage 2 add these with the apricots and butter to your basic bread mix.

Carry on through the basic recipe until Stage 5. I normally divide this dough into 4 and roll out into rolling-pin-shaped pieces and put these next to each other on a flour-dusted baking tray, but there's nothing stopping you cooking them in any shape. Allow the dough to double in size, then dust it with flour on the top and place it in your preheated oven at 180°C/350°F/gas 4 for around 30 minutes until lightly golden. Allow to cool for half an hour before using. Fantastic with cheese and Branston pickle.

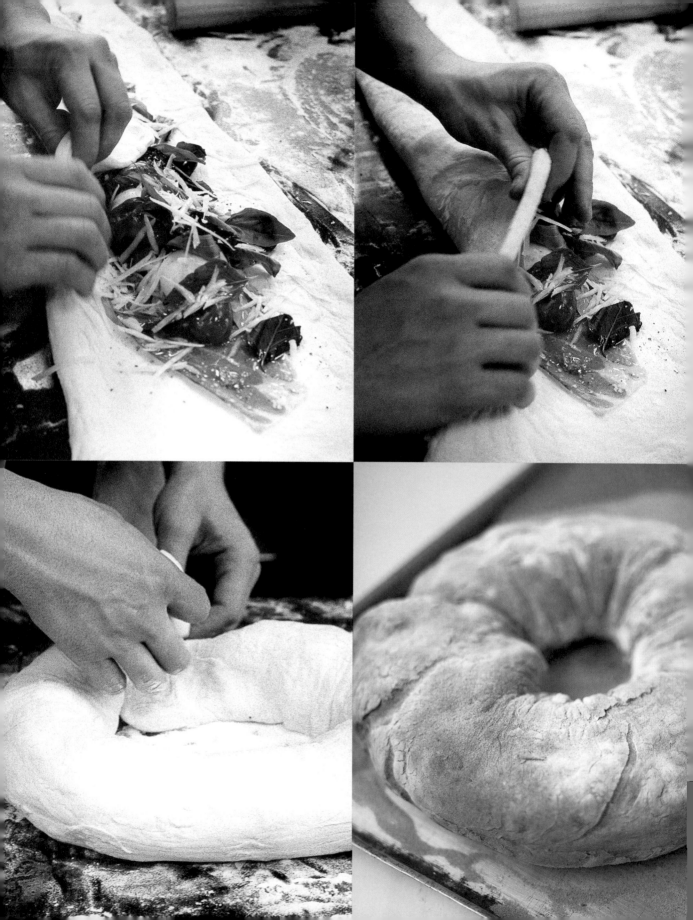

Rolled Bread of Parma Ham, Nice Cheese, Egg and Basil

1 x basic bread recipe (see page 236) • 10 slices of Parma ham
• 8 large organic eggs, boiled for 8 minutes and shelled •
400g/14oz cheese (a mixture of Cheddar, Fontina, Parmesan or
any leftovers that need to be used up), grated • 2 handfuls
of fresh basil • optional: sun-dried tomatoes or plum
tomatoes and olives, halved • extra virgin olive oil • sea salt
and freshly ground black pepper

Proceed through the basic bread recipe until Stage 5, dusting the dough with flour as you shape it into a long rectangle about 1cm/½ inch thick. This should end up being about 1 metre/39 inches long and about 18–20cm/7 or 8 inches wide.

Along the middle of the bread, lay out your Parma ham, eggs, cheese, basil and tomatoes and olives if you're using them. Drizzle with extra virgin olive oil and season with salt and pepper. Pull the dough over the filling so it forms what looks like a cannelloni shape. Then what you need to do is bring one end round to the other so that they join up. Pinch and pat the two ends together firmly to form a doughnut-shaped loaf. Transfer to a flour-dusted baking tin, allow to prove for 15 minutes, dust with flour and place in your preheated oven at 180°C/350°F/gas 4 for 35 minutes until golden. Allow to cool and then either transport to a picnic and carve it there – if you're lucky, it will still be a little warm in the middle – or eat there and then. Fantastic.

Courgette Bread

1 x basic bread recipe (see page 236) • 6 large
courgettes, washed and grated using a cheese grater •
1 small handful of fresh thyme, washed and leaves
picked • 200g/7oz goat's cheese, crumbled

At Stage 1 of the basic bread recipe, add 285ml/½ pint of your water along with the courgettes and thyme. Mix around, using your hands to scrunch the bread together – you'll find that water will come out of the courgettes so you may not need to add the rest of your water at Stage 2, but add some if you feel the dough needs it. Carry on with the basic recipe up to Stage 5 until the dough is elastic and not sticky. Then knead in the goat's cheese – it's an excellent combination. I normally shape the dough into a big round loaf and dust it with flour. Place on a flour-dusted baking tray and prove until doubled in size. Bake in your preheated oven at 180°C/350°F/gas 4 for around half an hour until crusty and hollow-sounding when tapped. It's superb toasted with cream cheese or just used as a normal sandwich bread.

Onion Baguettes

MAKES 4–6

1 x basic bread recipe (see page 236) • olive oil • 2 cloves of garlic, peeled and sliced • 1 handful of fresh thyme, washed and leaves picked • 3 white onions, finely sliced • sea salt and freshly ground black pepper • a splash of white wine vinegar

Into a pot, put 4 good lugs of olive oil, your sliced garlic and the thyme. Then add your onions, cover, and cook for 4 or 5 minutes. By then the moisture will have come out of the onions, so remove the lid and slowly cook away the liquid for a minute so you're left with nice, translucent, tasty onions – don't let them colour. Season to taste and add a small splash of vinegar.

While the onions are cooking, make your dough and continue through the basic bread recipe until Stage 5 where you divide your dough into 4 or 6 pieces, dust with flour, and roll into classic baguette shapes. Move them to a flour-dusted baking tray, then rub the onion mixture over the top of each baguette. Allow to prove until doubled in size, then bake in your preheated oven for 15 minutes at 180°C/350°F/gas 4 until the bread is crisp and lightly golden. The onions usually do burn a bit at the end, but that's all part of it. They end up being lovely. This is a fantastic sweet-tasting bread which is just nice, quite frankly, in a basket in the middle of the table before you tuck into dinner but is also pretty good with anything.

Sweet Cherry Focaccia Breakfast Stylie

1 x basic bread recipe (see page 236) • 1kg/2lb 3oz ripe
cherries • 4 heaped tablespoons vanilla sugar •
115g/4oz butter

Remove the pips from your cherries, either using your hands and simply pulling the pip out or using a cherry or olive pipper – this can be a little bit mucky and might stain your shirt, so put a pinny on. Once you've disposed of all the pips, sprinkle 2 tablespoons of the vanilla sugar over the cherries and put to one side while you make your bread dough.

Work through the basic bread recipe to Stage 5, when you're shaping the bread. You can divide the dough into two if you want to make 2 smaller ones. Push or roll out the dough to about 4cm/1½ inches thick. You can make them into rounds or fill a rectangular flour-dusted baking tray – it's up to you. Then you need to divide the cherries equally on to the dough and push them in and around as you would do with a normal focaccia – pushing your fingers right down to the bottom of the dough and sort of curling them under. Do this for about 2 minutes, then sprinkle your remaining sugar over the bread. Break your butter up into little knobs and put these on top. Leave to double in size, then place in the preheated oven at 180°C/350°F/gas 4 for around 25–30 minutes until slightly coloured and the bread is cooked. Best served slightly warm with more fresh butter and a cup of milky coffee. It's also absolutely fantastic kept in chunks in the freezer and reheated in the oven with vanilla ice cream on top, as a dessert. Yum yum.

Sourdough Bread

Sourdough is the original, truly natural bread. We are talking biblical stuff here, because instead of using commercial yeast, we are making bread with natural yeasts from the air. Over the last year, my Aussie chef friend Bernie and I have been on a mission to bake the perfect sourdough bread and I think we've cracked it. Knotty and chewy with a holey texture and awesomely crisp crust, which keeps the moistness inside, sourdough is the ultimate loaf. The method stretches over a week – but once you've got your starter mix, you can make it every day.

It's worth knowing that you should use organic rye flour on the first day as it contains wild yeast and bacteria and also that any additives or chemicals can stunt the growth of the microflora (a bit technical, but I thought you'd like to know!).

Monday Mix 500g/1lb 2oz of organic rye flour with enough water to make a soft dough, in a bowl. Put it outside for an hour, then bring it inside to a warm place and cover with clingfilm.

Tuesday It will start to bubble. Leave it alone.

Wednesday The mix will continue to bubble and will go slightly grey. At this point, stir in a handful of flour and little bit of water, enough to get the mixture back to the same consistency as on Monday. Leave it again, still covered.

Thursday Leave it alone.

Friday afternoon By now, you'll have a beery, malty-smelling, ashy-coloured mixture, full of natural yeasts, with loads of character. Make your bread by adding all of this starter dough mix to 1kg/2lb 3oz strong flour, then adding enough water to make a firm, pliable dough that is not sticky. Knead it for a good 5 minutes. Remove a 500g/1lb 2oz piece of dough for your next starter *before* adding any salt, cover and put to one side, ready to repeat the process the next day, and so on, etc.

Add salt if you want to. Shape the dough and put it into a bowl or tin lined with a floured tea-towel. Leave for 14 hours.

Saturday morning Bake the bread. Preheat the oven to 190ºC/375ºF/gas 5. Gently turn the dough out on to a floured baking tray, cut quite deep slashes into it, and bake for 1 hour or until it is crisp and sounds hollow when tapped on the bottom. Allow to cool and enjoy fresh, or grilled as crostini. When it is stale, rip it up and add to soups.

DESSERTS A nice large dessert section this time as I've got a bit of a sweet tooth at the moment. I've included quite a few comforting recipes like Lovely Lemon Curdy Pud and Fruit Cobbler. All sorts of things to suit sweet-freaks.

I must tell you a really sweet story about one of my recipes from *The Naked Chef*. At the end of my fruit crumble recipe I had added, 'I bet you have loads of your own ideas – try them.' I recently had a letter from an old lady who said she had tried to be a bit imaginative but the results didn't taste very nice. It turned out that she had put some paprika crisps in the crumble mix. That really did make me laugh, but it's nice to think that there are some seriously adventurous birds out there!

Pukka Pineapple with Bashed-up Mint Sugar

As a child I always thought that a simple fruit option for dessert was flippin' boring and it never excited me in the slightest. But I now realize it was because no one did anything remotely exciting with the fruit. This recipe, however, I would definitely have enjoyed as a kid. It's one of those combinations that just explodes in your mouth and you can't get enough of it. Once you try it, you'll never forget it.

SERVES 4

1 ripe pineapple • optional: natural yoghurt, to serve •
4 heaped tablespoons caster sugar • 1 handful of fresh mint

Buy yourself a ripe pineapple. It should smell slightly sweet and you should be able to remove the leaves quite easily. Cut both ends off and peel the skin with a knife, removing any little black bits. Then cut the pineapple into quarters and remove the slightly less tasty core, which I usually discard or suck on while preparing the rest of the dish. Finely slice your quarters, lengthways, as thin as you can. Lay out flat in one or two layers on a large plate. Don't refrigerate this – just put it to one side.

Take the plate to the table after dinner with a pot of yoghurt that can be passed round, then return with a pestle and mortar with the sugar in it. Your family or guests will probably think you've gone mad, especially if you ignore them while you do this, but pick the mint leaves and add them to the sugar. Bash the hell out of it in the pestle and mortar at the table. You'll see the sugar change colour and it will smell fantastic. It normally takes about a minute to do if you've got a good wrist action. Sprinkle the mint sugar over the plate of pineapple – making sure you don't let anyone nick any pineapple before you sprinkle the sugar over. What a fantastic thing. If you have any leftovers, you could always make a piña colada with them.

Cannoli Siciliana

This is a great little dessert that my mate Gennaro Contaldo, the Italian stallion, taught me to make. Cannoli biscuits are filled with lovely sweet ricotta and can be flavoured with absolutely anything. They can even be dipped into melted chocolate. You can buy them pre-made from all good Italian delis and most good supermarkets (if they haven't got them then tell them to order them in). They are basically deep-fried, sweetened pasta biscuits which are really light and crispy. These little babies keep well in the cupboard waiting to be turned into a great dessert that takes no time at all.

SERVES 4

2 large punnets of raspberries • 6 heaped tablespoons vanilla sugar • 200g/7oz ricotta cheese (buffalo is best) • 100g/3½oz good plain chocolate, chopped • 50g/1¾oz pistachio nuts, chopped • 50g/1¾oz glacé fruit, chopped • 12 cannoli biscuits • icing sugar

I love to make a raspberry sauce to go with these cannoli biscuits – just throw the raspberries into a small pan with 3 tablespoons of the sugar, bring to the boil, simmer for 1 minute then allow to cool.

Meanwhile, put your ricotta and the remaining 3 tablespoons of sugar into a Magimix food processor and blitz for 1 minute until shiny and smooth. If you taste the ricotta now it should be beautifully sweet. Some ricottas need more sugar than others, so taste and adjust to your preference. Scoop it out into a bowl and add your chocolate, pistachios and glacé fruit. Feel free to improvise with flavours here – you can only learn by trying. Put the mixture into a piping bag and pipe all the way through your cannoli biscuits. You can cut a small corner off a plastic or sandwich bag if you haven't got a piping bag. Place 3 biscuits on each plate, drizzled with your raspberry sauce and sprinkled with a little icing sugar. Lovely.

Yoghurt with Blueberry Jam and Elderflower Cordial

This is a fantastic quick recipe for those days when you don't want to spend ages knocking up a dessert. Or it can be a really good intermediate palate cleanser before your main course. It can be made with any jam you like, but blueberry jam is particularly tasty. Try strawberry or raspberry too.

SERVES 4

1 x 500g/1lb 2oz pot of good-quality Greek or natural yoghurt • 4 tablespoons blueberry jam • 8 tablespoons elderflower cordial • 4 sprigs of fresh mint

Divide your yoghurt between 4 dessert bowls or small glasses. Spoon over your blueberry jam, cover with your elderflower cordial, and top with a sprig of mint.

Fruit Cobbler

This is a fantastic American recipe equivalent to our crumble. Particularly good with strawberries and rhubard, but you can use any fruit combo you like; about 680g/1½lb of fruit should do it.

SERVES 6

FOR THE FRUIT

2 apricots, stoned and sliced • 1 pear, cored and thickly sliced •
1 punnet of blackberries • 1 punnet of blueberries • 1 punnet
of raspberries • ½ an apple, grated • 5 tablespoons sugar •
a good glug of balsamic vinegar

FOR THE TOPPING

170g/6oz butter, chilled • 225g/8oz self-raising flour •
70g/2½oz sugar • a large pinch of salt •
130ml/4½fl oz buttermilk • a little extra sugar for dusting

Preheat the oven to 190°C/375°F/gas 5. Put the fruit into a pan with the sugar and the balsamic vinegar, put the pan over the heat, and cook gently until the juices begin to run from the berries. Pour into an ovenproof dish.

Meanwhile make the topping. Rub the cold butter into the flour until the mixture resembles fine breadcrumbs. Add the sugar and salt, stir well, then add the buttermilk to form a loose scone-type mixture. Spoon this over the hot fruit (to get a cobbled effect, flick balls of dough randomly over the fruit), sprinkle with a little caster sugar, and bake in your preheated oven for 30 minutes until golden brown. Serve with vanilla ice cream.

Chocolate Cambridge Cream

Cambridge cream is basically a very similar recipe to crème brûlée. Feel free to double or even treble the recipe if you need to.

SERVES 4

3 vanilla pods • 200ml/7fl oz milk • 375ml/13fl oz double cream • 8 large egg yolks, preferably organic • 70g/2½oz caster sugar • 1 heaped teaspoon cocoa powder • 100g/3½oz good-quality chocolate, bashed up finely • extra sugar for caramelizing

Run your knife along the length of the vanilla pods, scraping out the seeds, then chop up the pods. Put the seeds and pods into a thick-bottomed pan with the milk and cream. Simmer slowly for 5 minutes for the flavour to infuse. In a bowl that will fit your pan, whisk the egg yolks, sugar and cocoa powder for a minute. Still slowly whisking, add the vanilla-flavoured milk and cream and keep whisking until well mixed. Add 2.5cm/1 inch of hot water to your dirty pan, bring to a simmer, and put your bowl on top of the pan. Cook the custard slowly over the simmering water for 5 minutes, stirring often, until it coats the back of a spoon. Get a jug, then push the custard through a fine sieve into it to remove the vanilla pods. Discard these.

Preheat your oven to 150°C/300°F/gas 2. Put 4 ovenproof serving dishes in a high-sided roasting tray. Divide your chocolate between them and shake flat. Carefully divide your custard mix between your dishes, making sure the chocolate isn't disturbed. Fill the tray with water until it is about half-way up the sides of your dishes. Cook in your preheated oven for around 30–45 minutes until slightly wobbly in the middle. Keep your eyes peeled and don't let the custards cook solid – remember that all ovens cook differently. Allow to cool (you can refrigerate these for up to 3 days if you like, but I like it best on the night at room temperature), then sprinkle with some sugar and caramelize with one of those small blowtorches (or you can boil 6 or 7 tablespoons of sugar with a couple of tablespoons of water until you have golden caramel and carefully pour this over the top if you're stuck).

Sesame Seed Toffee Snaps

These are great to mop up the lovely chocolate mousse on page 278. Caramel can cause quite bad burns, so keep your eyes peeled – even though this is a kids' favourite, you don't want to get kids involved in cooking this one.

MAKES ABOUT 12

455g/1lb caster sugar • 200g/7oz pack of sesame seeds

Put your sugar and 8–10 tablespoons of water into a pan on a medium heat. Use a spoon to stir together – it will become a syrup. Carry on cooking until light golden (but don't stir too much at this stage or sugar crystals will form in your syrup and you don't want this to happen), then add your sesame seeds and continue to cook until dark golden. Pour out your sesame seed caramel on to an oiled non-stick tray. Use a palette knife to push it out to about 0.5cm/¼ inch thick (even thinner if you can). Allow to cool for about 15 minutes and you will have one big sesame seed caramel biscuit. Bash it up as you like.

Cheeky Chocolate Mousse

SERVES 4

225g/8oz good-quality dark chocolate, bashed up • 70g/2½oz butter,
cut into pieces • 350ml/12fl oz double cream • 2 large eggs, preferably
organic • 1 tablespoon of Amaretto • 2 tablespoons good honey

In a bowl over some gently simmering water, slowly melt the chocolate and butter together then remove from the heat. In a separate bowl, semi-whip the cream (until soft peaks; not too stiff). In a third bowl, whisk the eggs and honey until light and fluffy then fold in the Amaretto, melted chocolate mixture and cream — gently, so you don't lose too much air. Pour into some small wineglasses or serving dishes and leave to chill for at least an hour before serving. Preferably serve with Sesame Seed Toffee Snaps (see page 275).

Chocolate and Whole Orange Pudding

A pudding with a lovely surprise in the centre of it when you cut it open. The orange peel is cooked like marmalade and its sharpness goes well with the sweetness of the chocolate.

SERVES 6–8

85g/3oz butter • 55g/2oz dark chocolate • 170g/6oz self-raising flour • 55g/2oz cocoa powder • 170g/6oz caster sugar • 2 eggs • 2 tablespoons milk

FOR THE FILLING

1 orange – preferably a thin-skinned navel variety • 85g/3oz butter • 85g/3oz caster sugar

First, bring some water to the boil in a pan (in which you are later going to steam your pudding), and put in your whole orange to boil fast for at least 10 minutes with the lid on.

Meanwhile, grease a 1.3 litre/2 pint pudding basin. Melt the butter with the chocolate in a bowl set over a pan of hot water. Put the flour and cocoa into a mixing bowl; add the melted butter and chocolate, then the sugar, eggs and milk, and mix well. Put about two-thirds of the mixture into the basin, making a well in the middle.

By this time the orange should have been boiling for about 10 minutes, and the peel should be nice and soft. Remove it carefully from the water. Prick the orange all over with a fork or skewer and place it in the middle of the pudding mix. You can (with care, as it's still hot) cut the orange into segments, if you want to check for pips or cut off the stringy bits of orange in the middle, then put it back together again (it does make it easier for serving), although I don't usually bother.

Dice the butter and dot it round the orange with the sugar, then cover with the remaining pudding mixture. Cover the pudding with greaseproof paper, then with tin-foil, and place in the pan of boiling water (it should come half-way up the sides of the basin). Steam for 2 hours. Don't forget to check now and then to see if the water needs topping up.

Turn the pudding out on to a serving dish and serve with custard or cream.

King of Puddings

SERVES 4–6

4 eggs • 565ml/1 pint milk • 115g/4oz fine
breadcrumbs • 225g/8oz sugar
(preferably vanilla sugar) • 4 level tablespoons jam
(raspberry is really nice)

Preheat the oven to 150°C/300°F/gas 2. Separate 3 of the eggs. Put the yolks into a bowl with the remaining whole egg and beat together. Add the milk, bread-crumbs and 85g/3oz of the sugar. Put the jam on the bottom of a pie dish and spread it evenly. Pour the custardy egg and milk mixture over the jam. Bake in your preheated oven for 1 hour or until set.

Whisk the remaining 3 egg whites until stiff, then slowly add the remaining sugar until it is all mixed in. Pile it on top of the custard, then bake in the oven for a further 15–20 minutes until the meringue is set and lightly browned.

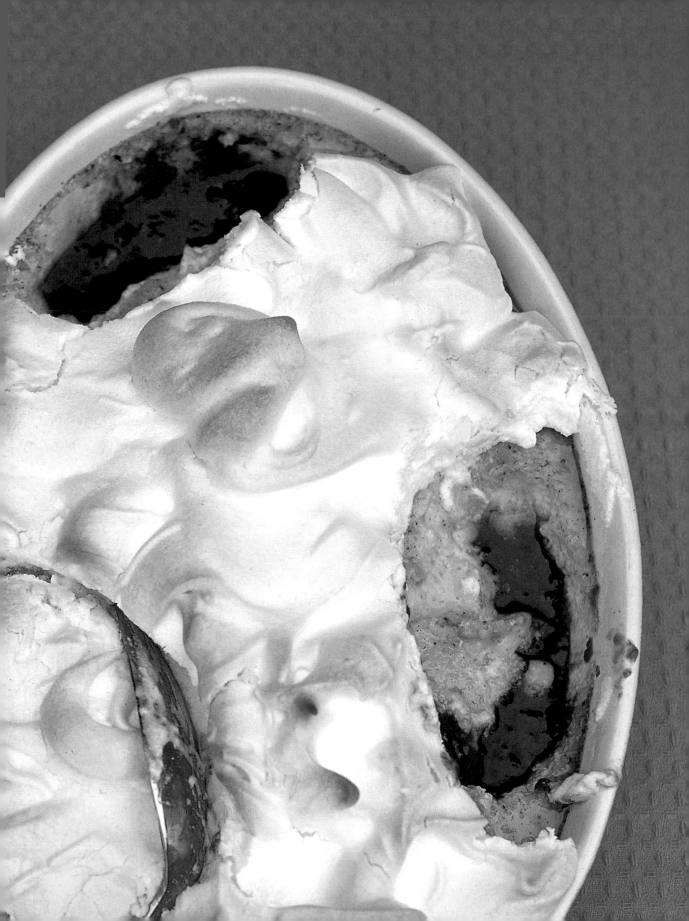

Lovely Lemon Curdy Pud

This is really tasty and dead easy to make – my sister Anna loves it! It looks good cooked in a Pyrex dish, as it goes into layers as it cooks, with a sort of lemon curdy custard at the bottom and a spongy meringuey top. Mmmmmmm … very delicious!

SERVES 4

55g/2oz butter • 115g/4oz sugar (vanilla sugar is nice) •
grated rind and juice of 1 lemon • 2 large eggs, separated
• 55g/2oz self-raising flour • 285ml/½ pint milk

Preheat the oven to 200°C/400°F/gas 6. Cream the butter, sugar and lemon rind in a mixing bowl. Add the egg yolks and flour and beat in, then add the milk and 3 tablespoons of lemon juice and mix well.

Whisk the egg whites in a separate bowl until stiff, then add the rest of the mixture. Mix it all well but don't over-mix it; you don't want the air to come out of the egg whites. Pour into a buttered ovenproof dish, stand the dish in a roasting tin about a third full of water, then bake in your preheated oven for about 45 minutes until the top is set and spongy and it's a nice golden colour.

Summer Fruit, Elderflower and Prosecco Jelly

This is a great dessert that is really tasty. It freshens the palate and you can make it before you need it – it keeps for about 4 or 5 days. You can make one large jelly in a tureen mould or dish, or you can do individual ones. Use any combination of fruit, but not pineapple or kiwi fruit, as the jelly won't set if you do.

SERVES 10

8 punnets of mixed soft fruit (blackberries, raspberries, strawberries, blueberries) • 4 leaves of gelatine • 140ml/¼ pint elderflower cordial • 2 heaped tablespoons caster sugar • 425ml/¾ pint prosecco (sparkling Italian wine), chilled

First of all, decide whether you want to make one big jelly or small individual ones. If you are making a big one, it's a good idea to line it with clingfilm. Put your ripe fruit into your mould or moulds and refrigerate. Put your gelatine leaves into a bowl with a little cold water to soak for a minute, then drain and add the gelatine back to the bowl with the cordial. Rest above a pan of water over a medium heat and stir constantly until the gelatine and cordial become a syrup. At this point you can add your sugar, stir till dissolved, then remove the bowl from the heat and let it sit at room temperature for a minute or so.

Take your fruit and prosecco out of the fridge. The idea being that your fruit, moulds and prosecco are all chilled, so the bubbles stay in the jelly when it sets and they fizz in your mouth when you eat it – beautiful! Pour the prosecco into your cordial mix, and then pour this over your fruit. Some of the fruit might rise to the top, so using your finger, just push the fruit down into the jelly mix so that it is sealed and will then keep well in the fridge. Put back into the fridge for an hour to set.

To serve, dip your mould into a bowl of hot water to loosen the outside of the jelly, then turn it out on to a plate. Great served with a little crème fraîche but just as good on its own.

What a great tart – chewy, with a gorgeous combo of pinenuts and honey. It was introduced to me by one of my good mates, Jethro, who's my pastry chef at Monte's. I met him in Australia and he's always been good with tarts! Thanks, Jethro. 'You is the man.'

Jethro Tart

MAKES A 30CM/12 INCH TART

255g/9oz pinenuts • 255g/9oz butter • 255g/9oz caster
sugar • 3 large eggs, preferably organic •
4 tablespoons Greek fig tree honey, or any good honey
• 115g/4oz plain flour • a pinch of salt

FOR THE PASTRY

115g/4oz butter • 100g/3½oz icing sugar • a pinch
of salt • 225g/8oz plain flour • 2 egg yolks • 2 tablespoons
cold milk or water

You can make the pastry by hand or in a food processor. Cream together the butter, sugar and salt and then rub or pulse in the flour and egg yolks. When the mixture has come together, looking like coarse breadcrumbs, add the milk or water. Gently pat together to form a small ball of dough. Wrap and leave to rest for an hour.

Carefully cut thin slices of your pastry (or you can roll out if you prefer) and place in and around the bottom and sides of your 30cm/12 inch tin. Push the pastry together and level out and tidy up the sides. Cover and leave to rest in the freezer for about 1 hour. Preheat your oven to 180°C/350°F/gas 4, and bake the pastry for around 15 minutes until lightly golden. Reduce the oven temperature to 170°C/325°F/gas 3.

While the pastry is in the oven, toast the pinenuts under the grill. If you're like me you'll forget about them and they'll burn, so keep your eyes peeled – they don't take long to colour. Using a spatula, or a food processor, whip the butter and sugar until light and fluffy. Stir in your pinenuts, add the eggs one at a time, then fold in the honey, flour and salt. Spoon into the tart shell and bake for 30–35 minutes.

Great served with caramelized figs (grilled with a little sugar), crème fraîche and a little lemon thyme.

Pannacotta with Roasted Rhubarb

SERVES 4

70ml/2½fl oz milk • 2 vanilla pods, scored
and seeds removed • finely grated zest
of 1 lemon • 375ml/13fl oz double cream •
1½ leaves of gelatine, soaked in water •
70g/2½oz icing sugar • 200g/7oz rhubarb
• 2 tablespoons caster sugar •
1 thumb-sized piece of fresh ginger, peeled
and grated • 1 x 2.5 cm/1 inch cinnamon
stick • 115ml/4fl oz champagne, prosecco
or other sparkling wine

Put the milk, vanilla pods, vanilla seeds, lemon zest and half the cream into a small pan and slowly simmer for 10 minutes or until reduced by a third. Remove from the heat and stir in the soaked gelatine leaves until dissolved. Allow to cool a little, then place in the fridge, stirring occasionally until the mixture coats the back of a spoon. Remove the vanilla pods.

Whip together the icing sugar with the remaining cream. Mix the two cream mixtures together. Divide into 4 serving moulds (I use little moulds, espresso cups or small glasses). Cover and chill for at least an hour.

Meanwhile chop the rhubarb into 4cm/1½ inch pieces, sprinkle with the caster sugar and grill until lightly browned. Gently heat together the ginger, cinnamon and champagne or prosecco, then pour over the roasted rhubarb, cover, and leave for about 30 minutes for the flavours to do their bit.

To serve, sometimes I'll dip the mould or cup into some simmering water to loosen the pannacotta a little, then turn it out on to a plate next to some rhubarb with its juice (remove the cinnamon). Or you can just put the rhubarb on top of your cups or glasses of pannacotta and serve from there. Both ways are cool. Also gorgeous served with fresh figs and honey or caramelized blood oranges.

PS Nice with a little basil.

BEVVY BEVOIRES I'm still very partial to a good old drink. And it's nice to know that you lot are too. My lord, how people went mad for the vodka watermelon from *Return of the Naked Chef* – from teenagers to OAPs I wasn't sure who was worse. I even caught my mate Jimmy injecting passion fruit and grapes with vodka – what a nutter! You can tell he's a student. But if you want something to swear by this time, have a go at a Sidecar, which is my biggest luxury at the moment. Great for calming you down and kickstarting the night. Just to show that I'm not obsessed with cocktails, I've included some absolutely amazing soft drinks, including Christmas in a Glass, which is pure joy. It's mandarin juice with a little mint; my family drinks it on Christmas Day. And there's a quick recipe for ginger beer, which is the most refreshing thing to drink on a hot summer day. Have a look and have a drink on me.

bev

The Best Hot Chocolate

This is a great way to make the best hot chocolate, cappuccino or frothy milk drinks at home without having to buy any expensive machinery. All you need is a good-sized thermos flask or a plastic jug with a screw-top lid. I've even made pukka Ovaltine like this!

SERVES 2

565ml/1 pint full cream or semi-skimmed milk • 2 tablespoons best drinking chocolate • 1 handful of marshmallows • sugar to taste

This takes around 3 or 4 minutes to make. First put the milk into a pan. Bring to a simmer – not a boil – and while it's heating, put a tablespoon of choccie powder and sugar to taste into each mug. Add a little warmish milk from the pan to each mug – you just need enough to dissolve the chocolate powder. At this point, plonk a few marshmallows into each mug. When the milk is at a simmer, carefully pour it into a plastic jug or flask. I normally do this over a sink as I always end up spilling a bit (the trick is to have a big enough jug or flask so the milk only half fills it – you need the extra space for shaking and frothing).

Screw the lid on tightly, place a cloth over the lid for safety, and shake hard for a minute. Remove the lid, minding the steam, and pour the milk into your mugs. A little stir and you can slurp your way to heaven!

Easy Peasy Ginger Beer

Ginger beer is one of my favourite things in the world, especially blooming good in the summer when it's getting hot. I can't think of anything more sexy than having a big jug of iced ginger beer on the table with a barbecue on a hot day. The classic real ginger beers use a starter, and these are fantastic but slow, so here's my short-cut for getting amazing results taking hardly any time.

SERVES 4–6

140g/5oz fresh ginger • 4 tablespoons muscovado sugar •
2–3 lemons • 1 litre/1¾ pints soda water or sparkling mineral
water • sprigs of fresh mint

First of all you need to grate your ginger on a coarse cheese grater – you can leave the skin on if you like. Put the ginger with its pulpy juice into a bowl and sprinkle in your muscovado sugar. Remove the rind from 2 of your lemons with a vegetable peeler, add to the bowl, and slightly bash and squash with something heavy like a pestle or a rolling-pin. Just do this for 10 seconds, to mix up all the flavours. Squeeze the juice from all 3 lemons and add most of it to the bowl. Pour in your fizzy water or soda water. Allow to sit for 10 minutes and then taste. You may feel that the lemons are slightly too sour, therefore add a little more sugar; if it's slightly too sweet, add a little more lemon juice. To be honest, these amounts are always a little variable so just follow your own taste. Pass the ginger beer through a coarse sieve into a large jug and add lots of ice and some sprigs of mint.

Christmas in a Glass

Last Christmas we had so many tangerines and mandarins in the house, we knew that they were all going to go mouldy and dodgy. So we kept a few, then cut the rest in half and juiced them. Then we put the juice through a coarse sieve to remove any chunky pith and added a few mint leaves. We served this chilled on Christmas morning and it was an absolute joy. All we could say was that it was Christmas in a glass. Every time we took a sip it tasted like Christmas, if you can imagine what Christmas tastes like. But seriously, this is one of the best drinks that I've ever had. When mandarins, tangerines or clementines are in season and cheap, it's a great drink to use with maybe champagne, prosecco, in cocktails or just as juice on its own. Give it a try. You will need about 5 mandarins per person.

Mango Lassi

This Indian drink is like a mango milkshake and is delicious.

SERVES 4

255ml/9fl oz plain yoghurt • 130ml/4½fl oz milk •
130ml/4½fl oz canned mango pulp or 200g/7oz fresh mango,
stoned and sliced • 4 teaspoons sugar, to taste

Put all the ingredients into a blender and blend for 2 minutes, then pour into
individual glasses and serve. The lassi can be kept refrigerated for up to 24 hours.

Sidecar

This is a superb little cocktail and the recipe is from Tony Debok at a bar called Daddy-O in New York. Definitely one to try.

SERVES 1 (LARGE)

3 tablespoons caster sugar • 55ml/2fl oz good brandy • 20–25ml/¾fl oz Cointreau • 2 or 3 fresh limes, juiced • sugar and lime rind, to serve

First stir 3 tablespoons of sugar and 3 tablespoons of boiling water together until dissolved, then add the brandy, Cointreau and lime juice. Add some ice and shake well. Taste a little – you may want to add some more lime to give it an edge. Serve up in a martini glass with a sugar rim and a lime twist.

Margarita

SERVES 1

2 shots of tequila • 1 shot of Cointreau • 1 shot of freshly squeezed lime juice • salt and lime wedge, to serve

Put all the ingredients into a shaker. Shake well and serve in a martini glass with a salt rim and a split lime wedge.

MONTES
— 164 —
Jum and Bender

This great little cocktail was made by the barman after me and my mate Ben started working at Monte's.

SERVES 1

3 passion fruit • a little champagne to top up •
a dash of grenadine

Halve the passion fruit and push the juice through a coarse sieve to separate the lovely flavour from the seeds. Throw the seeds away but keep all the pulpy juice which will have gathered on the underside of the sieve. Pour into a tall glass and top up with champagne and a dash of grenadine. Cheers!

AND FINALLY . . .
YOU ARE WHAT YOU EAT

I recently met a fantastic lady called Jane Clarke who is a dietitian in Soho. In actual fact, she hates the word dietitian so she calls herself a 'food-loving nutritionist'. The thing I love about Jane is that she enjoys cooking with all kinds of flavours and she believes that a good diet isn't just about losing weight. If we eat well it will help us to feel livelier and more healthy, and can make us look better and even perform better at work. While I was chatting to Jane, she suggested a few things that we can all do in order to ensure that we eat a better diet. It's common-sense stuff that we can all benefit from, so check it out and have a go at some of these things.

- *Drink more water* It's good to have 2.5 litres/about 4½ pints a day. Water is great for fending off headaches, easing digestion, improving your skin and will give you more energy. It also helps to release all the vitamins and minerals from your food into your body. There's nothing wrong with drinking tap water – if you don't like the taste then get yourself a filter.

- *Eat slowly and enjoy your food* If you eat your food too quickly your brain won't pick up on the fact that you're actually full up as quickly as it should, so you will carry on stuffing yourself until you've eaten too much. Eating slowly will ensure that your brain tells you when you're full. It's the same if you eat food that doesn't have much flavour – your brain gets bored, switches off and doesn't tell you when you're full. Eat flavoursome food and listen to your brain! Talking of flavour, it's good to use herbs and spices to make food taste good – and that way you won't need to use too much salt.

- *Eat 'real' food rather than low-calorie food* This may surprise you, but a little bit of 'real' full-fat food is much better for you than many of the low-fat versions. Take low-fat chocolate, for example – this will usually have had something not so good added to it to compensate for the flavour that has been taken out along with the fat. To keep your heart healthy, use olive or vegetable oils rather than over-relying on butter.

- *Eat small meals often* Don't skip breakfast and stuff yourself at lunchtime or your food will sit heavily and overload your stomach.

- *Watch that you don't overdose on carbohydrates during the day* Since carbohydrates like pasta and potatoes activate your de-stressing hormones, they can make you feel relaxed and a bit dozy, which is why it may be better to eat them at the end of the day, when you want to unwind, rather than at lunchtime.

- *Resist alcohol on an empty stomach* This is a tip which I completely agree with (as I have done this and suffered the consequences!). It will send your energy levels crashing and you'll feel shattered as your blood sugar level is lower. You'll feel that you've got to eat something immediately – whether it be crisps, a doner kebab or a curry. It's much better to eat and drink at the same time which means you can still get tiddly but without all the negative effects on your digestive system. If you haven't got time, then a glass of milk or a banana before you start drinking should stop the alcohol having such a drastic effect.

- *Watch the caffeine* Things like coffee, tea and cola all contain caffeine. If you have too much the caffeine produces adrenalin which will stress you out even more. Stick to 2 or 3 cups of really good coffee, and then maybe drink herbal tea or hot water with a slice of ginger or lemon, which should help you feel calmer and sleep better.

- *Eat more protein* A lot of us don't eat enough protein: fish (especially the oily fish), eggs, seafood, lean meat, pulses, nuts, grains, etc. Protein gives us energy and is also good for controlling moods, because it contains things called amino acids which produce 'happy hormones' in our bodies which make us feel good. If you're feeling a bit down, try eating some protein to perk you up.

- *It's really worth eating lots of fruit and veg* Hopefully everyone knows that eating 5 portions of fruit and veg a day can help to prevent things like heart disease and cancer – find the ones you like, and work them into your diet. Tomatoes are so good for you and research shows they are good at protecting men from prostate cancer – apparently 10 portions a week can reduce the risk by up to 45 per cent. A portion is about 2 tomatoes – but you can easily get the equivalent, and more, probably, from a Bloody Mary, or a tomato sauce for pasta – or even ketchup!

Page numbers in **bold** denote illustrations
v indicates vegetarian recipe

NICE ONE GUYS I'd just like to say a special thanks to all the people who help me do what I do – all of whom are now great friends of mine. I'll start with my family … My amazing wife Jools for marrying me and putting up with me, to my gorgeous mum and dad as always for everything, to the rest of the Oliver, Palmer and Norton families for their support, especially that Mrs Qwwyyzzy Norton • David Loftus, the most talented and patient photographer I've ever known, a best mate and great travelling partner. Bring on the Sidecars bro! PS Much love to Debbie, Paros and Pascale • Thanks to my fantastic assistants Louise Holland, Nicola Duguid and Lisa Norton for your true dedication and friendship xxx • Thanks to my best friends for being my best friends: Andy the gasman, he's still single and available, Jimmy Doherty the nature boy, Dan Brightman the Cornish Surfer, and all the other nutters I grew up with, Willy Wilson, Gray Boy, Ruby Quince and the rest • To Gennaro and Liz and all of the Passione team in Charlotte Street for being like a second family xxx • All my love to my beloved Lindsey Jordan, my editor. And to Tom Weldon, my publisher, who has been surprisingly calm through the whole book! Thanks … what can I say? To Johnny Boy Hamilton for putting up with me being so intense over the design and look of the book, and for working around my mad life on Sundays and late nights I should thank your wife – really sorry, Claire. Massive respect to Jo Seaton, Annie Lee, Nicky Barneby, James Holland, Sophie Brewer, Tora Orde-Powlett, Keith Taylor, John Bond and Miss Moneypenny, Harrie 'she's free and available' Evans, Peter Bowron and all the brilliant Penguin sales team • Patricia Llewellyn, my TV producer and the infamous voice behind *The Naked Chef*, you are the best. Thanks for everything, Niall and Ewen, the directors of the programmes, and to the rest of the team – Peter Gillbe, Nina, Lucy, Rowan, Chris, Patrick, Jon, Louise, Luke Cardiff and Richard Hill • Mark Gray, Paul Hunt, Khoi, Josh and Tessa for all their work on jamieoliver.com • To the lovely Ginny Rolfe, wonder woman, and her fella John the baker • Kate Habershom • Harriet Docker • Richard at the Warehouse • Cheers to my agents, Borra, Aden, Michelle and Martine from Deborah McKenna Ltd • Lance Reynolds • Sheila Keeting, for being an absolute diamond • To lovely Lincoln, Jane and all the kids, Sunny, Jake and Honey, bless • Jane Clarke • To Uncle Geoff, Heather, Ashley and Stephanie • To my mate Bender the Aussie and all my chefs and managers at Monte's (164 Sloane Street, London SW1X 9QB. Telephone: 020 7235 0555) • To Mr Frost, the one who made me famous • To the mad liver lips Charlie, and to Maria for sorting me out big time • Thanks to Das and all the team from Rasa in London for their support and genius Indian food • And, last but not least, a massive thanks to my suppliers: To Patricia from La Fromagerie, the best cheese shop in the world • David Gleave from Liberty Wines (020 7720 5350) for helping me source some fantastic olive oils and wines from Italy • Jekka, the loveliest organic herb lady in the world. Get your window boxes done, www.jekkasherbfarm.com • Birgit Erath at the Spice Shop (www.thespiceshop.co.uk) • Everyone at Borough Market in London for their amazing Fridays and Saturdays – such passion and hard work; you make my weekends exciting. Here's to more markets like yours • To the best fishmongers … George at Golborne Fisheries, Ben at Rossmore Fisheries, The Southbank Seafood Company Ltd and John at Blagdens for his great game • The butchers: Kevin at Allen's, Brian at Randalls and Gary at M. Moen & Sons • Rushton, Greg and all the boys at George Allens Vegetables for all the early calls • Hyams and Cockerton for all the fruit and veg • To Sir Peter Davis and the Sainsbury's posse for letting me launch exciting projects like the herb range and here's to more in the future.

Sorted . . . I'm off